Southern Christmas Stories

Vicki H. Moss

GRACE
PUBLISHING

Scripture references are taken from *The Holy Bible, New International Version.*® Copyright © 1973, 1978, 1984 by International Bible Society. Used by permission of Zondervan. All rights reserved.

Typefaces used for the text of this book include Adobe Garamond Pro, Gabriola, and Bible Script. Cover fonts include Chopin Script, Constantina, and Times.

Southern Christmas Stories
ISBN 978-1-60495-113-4

Copyright © 2025 by Vicki H. Moss. Published in the U.S.A. by Grace Publishing, Broken Arrow, Oklahoma. All rights reserved. No part of this book may be reproduced in any form or by any electronic or mechanical means, including information storage and retrieval systems, without permission in writing from the author, except as provided by U.S.A. Copyright law.

The following stories were first published in books of the *Divine Moments* series, compiled by Yvonne Lehman and Terri Kalfas, published by Grace Publishing.

Divine Moments
"No Need to Fear Falling"

Christmas Moments
"A Christmas Point of View"
"Counting Southern Treasures"

More Christmas Moments
"Suzy Snowflake and the Blue Christmas that Turned White"

Additional Christmas Moments
"The Christmas Santa Died and Rudolph Became Toast"

Merry Christmas Moments
"Trinity's Grace"

Remembering Christmas
"The Life Saver of My Hard Candy Christmas"

'Tis the Season
"The Christmas Tree Skirt"

Dedicated to Kathy, Pete, Sarah, Suzanne, Tracy, Aunt Ruby and Uncle Tommy. Thanks for all of the wonderful memories!

Contents

1. The Life Saver of My Hard Candy Christmas 7
2. Christmas Redemption 13
3. Suzy Snowflake and the Blue Christmas that Turned White ... 18
4. The Christmas Santa Died and Rudolph Became Toast 25
5. Sashaying Through Aunt Ruby's Red Door 31
6. Dirty Santa 38
7. No Need to Fear Falling 42
8. A Christmas Point of View 48
9. The Christmas Tree Skirt 54
10. Counting Southern Treasures Through the First Noel 59
11. Trinity's Grace 66
12. The Big Apple Christmas Prequel 78
13. The Buyout 86
14. An Unforgettable Christmas 92
15. Snowing the Christmas Village 104
16. Sven and the Tornado 109
17. Red Velvet Cake 117
18. Stained Glass Ornaments 124
19. Nutcracker at the Tivoli 129
20. The Scent of Christmas 134
21. Santa's Big Question 138
22. Christmas on the River 139

~ 1 ~
The Life Saver of My Hard Candy Christmas

Christmas was coming in our second grade class. My classmates and I had already drawn names out of a bowl so we could exchange gifts before leaving school for our Christmas break. The dollar amount—or I should say less than dollar amount—to be spent on the Christmas gifts was to be fifty cents. And all of us kids knew what we all loved that cost fifty cents was a foldout book of candy Life Savers that held five rolls in each side of the book. My strategic plan for the big Christmas party was well thought out. I would buy a book of Life Savers for the name I drew and, hopefully, whoever drew my name would gift me with the same.

So excited, I could hardly wait for the party. Just thinking about having ten whole Life Savers packs, five nestled in each side of "the book," made my mouth water. I could make that candy last for a couple of weeks! Thinking myself fairly generous, I thought I might even give away the butterscotch roll to someone else, since it was Christmas and a time to be generous, and I wasn't all that fond of butterscotch anyway.

When it came time to go shopping for my school Christmas gift exchange, I told Mother what I needed. "Everyone will be giving books of Life Savers, and that's what I need to buy." At the grocery store, Mother needed to pick up a list of necessary items for holiday baking and I watched our shopping buggy fill as she chose a bag of assorted unshelled nuts for Daddy to eat—he had fun using the nutcracker—and then there were also the oranges and tangerines for the fruit basket that would make our home smell like Christmas, a pineapple for the Pineapple Upside Down Cake Mother would make which was only one of the many cakes she always baked, along with cocoa, lemon, and coconut for pies, cloves for scoring the ham, vanilla extract and eggs for cakes and snow cream—just in case it snowed, red coloring for the Red Velvet Cake, and shelled pecans for the cream cheese icing with extras for the fruitcake. Then there were a couple of five pound bags of sugar for the cakes, pies, and hot chocolate we had to have on cold nights, and of course a plump bag of marshmallows to float in the hot chocolate. And fudge. We couldn't forget the ingredients for the homemade fudge. An extra bag of sugar might be needed for extra snow cream "in case that big snow did come…."

I reminded Mother to get plenty of popcorn—which she loved more than anyone—for TV watching. But the best purchase of all was the red hard candy, shaped like a ribbon, that would reside for a short time in the ruby-red covered candy dish that graced an end table in the living room.

Not far from the hard ribbon candy, I spotted them on the grocery store shelf. The Life Savers. I added ribbon candy and a Life Savers "book" to the buggy and I was all set. Now, if only whoever drew my name at school was shopping for my same exact gift as well, my Christmas was pretty much going to be fantastic, that is until Santa Claus came and then it would hopefully be a dilly. I'd asked Santa for a doll house and had shared that request with my parents.

But there was one more errand to run. Mother was going to splurge! So we stopped by the Brock Candy Company—which we did every Christmas—to buy Daddy a box of chocolate covered cherries because number one: He loved them and it was Christmas. And number two: They were less expensive if bought at Brock Candy Company during the Christmas season.

The last day of school couldn't roll around fast enough for all of the excited grammar school children. Christmas party day had arrived. We sat four to a large table/desk anticipating receiving our presents. Full of laughter and anticipation, we were all punch-and-cupcake-giddy. The boy next to me ripped the paper off his package, and there it was—a book of Life Savers. I couldn't wait to get mine. Someone else at the table cried out in sheer delight over a similar Life Savers box, "Yes! This is just what I wanted!"

Then my gift was handed to me. A present from a little slip of a blonde-headed girl named Louise (not her real name), it was obvious the package was too thin to be a box of Life Savers and my heart sank down to my bee-bop shoes. No longer giddy, I tried holding my disappointment in check, and slowly unwrapped my gift. What I held in my hands could only be a book. I loved books. Right? But a book was even better if it had Life Savers in it!

What my eyes beheld was a small dime store book titled *The Night Before Christmas*. Santa Claus and his reindeer were on the front cover. Along with the price tag. Ten cents. Dime, indeed. Louise hadn't even spent the amount suggested by the teacher. I already knew this story, practically by heart. Babies knew this story. I felt like I had never been so cheated. While almost everyone else was enjoying the sweetness of a Life Saver, I was enjoying the sourness of disappointment and hurt feelings. Why couldn't someone else have drawn my name?

Only seven years old, I tried to regroup, and muster up some manners. Before leaving school, I thanked Louise for my gift though I doubt the smile on my face was genuine, or even if I wore a smile. Later, I tried my best to sort it all out. Why me Lord? Why couldn't Louise have drawn someone else's name? There was all my hurt laid out before the Lord. And my disappointment. Louise drawing my name was the unluckiest incident ever! And though I hadn't yet turned my life over to the Lord with being "saved" and being immersed in a public baptism, the Lord was speaking to me even then.

What was brought to my mind was that somehow—maybe some of the other children knew and had told me—I knew Louise was living with grandparents who were rearing her and a younger sister and they obviously lived on a limited income. They were poor. No one knew anything about Louise's biological parents or where they were in the scheme of things. That part was a mystery. When it came to material things, Louise and her sister seemed less fortunate than some of the rest of us. None of us were wealthy, but most of us had enough. And I knew in my heart of hearts that by the way Louise and her tiny waif of a sister dressed, they could have used a little more.

And my heart began to soften. After all, I reasoned, I could always have one of Daddy's chocolate covered cherries. He didn't mind sharing with me. And Mother would soon have those cakes and pies baked. And how could I forget? I had assorted nuts and oranges and tangerines waiting for me in my living room not far away from the ruby-red covered dish that held ribbon shaped hard candy. Maybe this entire Christmas was going to be a hard candy Christmas. Maybe Santa would pull through. Maybe not. He was sometimes a disappointment too, bringing the wrong toys. Hard candy Christmas or not, there might still be a big snow. There would always be cakes and pies, and even if there was no snow and no sugar involved, being with my cousins was wonderful. Plenty of sugar was to be had for all by kissing the chubby cheeks of the family babies.

During Christmas break, even though I was familiar with *The Night Before Christmas,* I memorized the story word for word so I could recite it to my younger kin to make the holidays more fun. And a fun Christmas we had, while celebrating the birth of the Savior.

Years later, when going off to college and trying to weed out some of the things I'd managed to hoard through the years, I couldn't let go of that little book so long ago received from Louise during the second grade Christmas party. So I kept it long into adulthood.

It would be many years later when I ran across *The Night Before Christmas* and thought about that year's Christmas party incident with the lack of Life Savers. And it dawned on me that the Lord, in His sovereign mercy, allowed my disappointment so I could experience one of the best celebrations of all. He had taught me it was better to give than to receive. I'd learned that though a gift might be small and thin and not as costly as some, it could be one of the most treasured gifts for years to come with lessons to be passed down to future generations. That Christmas, and unknowingly, Louise gave me a gift that would teach me one of the best lessons I'd ever learn. To be humble and to be kind. What an event to celebrate with at least a cake!

When I think about Louise today, I pray she has had a blessed life with many uplifting moments—that she was successful and productive with many children of her own to nourish and love.

The most important lesson from that year: Jesus Christ taught me He was the real Life Saver—the Life Saver of my hard candy Christmas, the Life Saver of eternal life—a lesson I will always thank Him for and treasure in my heart.

*Whoever humbles himself like this child
is the greatest in the kingdom of heaven.*

Matthew 18:4 NIV

Consider it all joy, my brethren, when you encounter various trials.

James 1:2 KJV

*In everything I did, I showed you that by this kind of hard work
we must help the weak, remembering the words the Lord Jesus,
himself said, "It is more blessed to give than to receive!"*

Acts 20:35 NIV

~ 2 ~
Christmas Redemption

Twas the Christmas Uncle Jimmy said, "If I'd had a boy like that, I'd kill him." Several Christmas-light gawkers driving through the neighborhood reported brother *already* dead.

But allow me to back up with some backstory. The beginning of this tale proved even more tragic:

Growing up in my neighborhood, there were many non-working mothers with time on their hands. Many were Garden Club members who—since they made the list themselves—had first dibs on the Christmas songs each family would choose from for a theme to decorate their homes. The "best decorated house" award, according to a vote, was presented yearly. By the time my family saw the songs left on the list, all of the good songs had been taken. The best songs were:

"Santa Claus Is Coming to Town"—a no-brainer. Everybody had a fake Santa laying around.

"Jingle Bells"—a breeze.

"Suzy Snowflake"—bummer—the leftover Mom brought home. Served up cold. Who even knew the tune?

We held a family pow-wow.

Brother's idea: My three-year-old doll, Darlene, could play Suzy. Her job: Stand in the frigid snow by the "Suzy Snowflake" sign. With a smile on her face.

Mom said, "Great idea! We'll change the foil color we normally use to present-wrap the door, and then hang the silver bells. That will also change our decorations up some."

Dad boasted, "I'll nail fake Santa's sled and reindeers to the roof and we can throw some wrapped packages in the sleigh."

Sis gushed, "The mailbox needs sprouting greenery and singing bells! The cedar and shrubs must twinkle!" (Or something like that.)

Brother snorted in glee because my favorite doll—my run-to girl when everyone in the family picked on me and I had no one else to turn to—would be exposed to the elements.

I blurted out, "No way!"

Everyone else jingled with holiday spirit while eating tangerines and nuts while I fumed. The family cut a deal: I could bring Darlene back inside after traffic died down to warm her up until the next evening when all of the Christmas lookers began driving by again.

What would really pacify me? An acoustic guitar. The year before, I'd penciled it on the Santa list.

Santa had Alzheimer's that year.

I'd stormed back to bed. Sobbed. Wailed. Pillow-punched. And sobbed some more.

The jolly fat man had also failed to assemble my Barbie Dream House. The guy wearing the flashy-red suit didn't have the first hint of carpentry skills. Even while wearing coke-bottle thick glasses, he reeked of incompetence.

Santa had one last chance.

The deal about the use of Darlene for Suzy Snowflake agreed upon, we were all now ready to dream big.

Mother had been hinting for months she'd like to have a bottle of White Shoulders perfume.

Daddy was always happy with chocolate-covered cherries. Anything that topped those cherries was pure gravy for him.

Brother? Who cared! Pondering long, I bought a canned hockey player puzzle. Wrapped it. Scribbled his name on the tag.

Christmas Eve found us rattling presents, sucking ribbon candy, slurping cinnamon-laced wassail, crooning along with Alvin and the Chipmunks, belting out, "…please Christmas don't be late."

All except Brother. Trust me, no one missed him when the front door had been locked for the night.

DING! DONG! Now, who could that be at this late hour?

Upon opening the door, my parents were faced with a stranger standing next to Brother who was trying to dust snow from his jeans. "Son!" the stranger said. "You okay? I thought you'd been electrocuted by the spotlight wires!"

Outside, Brother had been fake-dying, casting shadows against the side of the neighbor's house so he could watch himself slowly die and fall to the ground, then snow-writhe while pretending electrocution. After dying, he'd bounce back to life. To die all over again. All this while automobiles turtle-crawled up the street ringing out snow chain music.

What Brother hadn't counted on, was someone thinking he really *had* been electrocuted. The poor motorist had thrown his car into park, leaving his family with the car door open while they shivered in arctic air blasts, while he ran to rescue Brother. Which caused traffic to back up from Tennessee to the gulf.

After the man was reassured that, "It was only a game. I was just foolin,' practicing my dying skills," and the door was shut, the earth quaked. How could Christmas get any worse?

Yet, it did. Christmas morning, Mother opened *four* bottles of White Shoulders. Maybe that wasn't such a bad thing. Now she had a life's supply and our living room smelled aromatic.

But then Sis opened a present that was not to her liking.

Dad's underwear was too small.

My guitar? Electric. No amplifier. What?!

Santa was a schmuck.

Suzy Snowflake? Simply a loser through no fault of her own and left out in the cold.

And all of this tragedy happening while brother sat on the sofa tripping unsuspecting passersby—yet somehow he always managed to either redeem or resurrect himself. How was I born into this family?

So much for the holidays.

At twilight, however, I, the angelic chosen child, stood before succulent turkey and sweet potato pie and prepared to read Luke's version of Jesus' birth to extended family. I was praying for my rapture right after the nativity story and mouthed a heartfelt "Jesus come quickly," because presents had already been opened and I'd been utterly disappointed.

Later, after the feast disappeared from the table, Brother worked on the hockey player puzzle I'd gifted him.

Uncles conspicuously strolled by on their way for their sixth helping of chocolate and lemon pie while surreptitiously glancing over to the table and eying the hockey player taking shape. I could hear their snickering before I saw grins.

Last piece in to the puzzle, there were no pucks! Maybe no

one was looking for a puck because Miss August looked nothing like a hockey player. Hmmmm. The puzzle wasn't a sports puzzle but more like—why was she wearing bunny ears—a Playboy bunny puzzle? All eyeballs turned my way and the looks said, *Is this revenge for Darlene having to stand out in the cold to play-act she is Suzy Snowflake?*

How was I ever going to live this down? And how was I to know about the puzzle? It had a hockey player on the outside of the can so I, um, *thought* it was a hockey player. What a disaster of a holiday.

Mom took a break from the kitchen long enough to see what all the chuckles were about and at last made sure the puzzle quickly disappeared. For good.

Oh…and the best gift I received from Mother that year was only a raised eyebrow.

Looking back over the years, I recount the many Christmas mishaps, blunders and disappointments—and with every one, I wouldn't trade one Christmas memory for a bucket of diamonds.

And Darlene? She wore angel wings when I had my own home, though she was missing part of her index finger. A certain daughter was cutting her back molars and had a teething frenzy before I could get Darlene to safety. Darlene remained stoic as ever.

And welp, during Darlene's retirement years, she was still a good sport about everything and stood at the top of the staircase overlooking golden angels flying below my crystal chandelier in the foyer. Of course the golden flying angels had a little help from fishing line that could hardly be detected and they didn't mind Darlene standing above them, sometimes directing their flight patterns.

~ 3 ~

Suzy Snowflake and the Blue Christmas that Turned White

Guess I'm still not done talking about Darlene being volunteered to be Suzy Snowflake. There's more. I probably should have gone to a therapist about the Suzy Snowflake incident, but back then kids just toughed out their trauma.

The front door had been wrapped like a present and was garnished with silver bells and a bow. All of our received Christmas cards had been taped on the inside of the door to form a Christmas tree. A pine tree's scent permeated the entire house while red, blue, and yellow bubble lights rested on limbs of evergreen glittering with silver icicles and holding more than one ornament. Striped ribbon candy decorated ruby red dishes not far from a basket laden with crisp apples, oranges, and mixed nuts waiting to be cracked to reveal tasty meats. Elvis could be heard crooning "Blue Christmas" from the stereo. "I'll uh have uh uh-a Bluuuuue Christmas, without you…."

In the dining room, the table was graced with a nutmeg-scored ham straight from the oven and groaned even more from the weight of vegetables, rolls, cakes, and pies of all shapes and sizes; all made from scratch at the request of family members.

Outside, the doll I'd named Darlene—the doll who was

my childhood best friend—was on display next to the sign in the front yard: "Suzy Snowflake." That song title had been one of the few Christmas song titles left for Mother to choose from the neighborhood garden club's list residents were supposed to use that year for decorations. As I mentioned before, songs like "Jingle Bells," "Away in a Manger," and "Silver Bells"—all titles that would have been easy to find decorations for—had been taken first by those women who participated in the garden club. Because Mother worked and couldn't attend meetings which were held during work hours, the titles left to choose from were slim pickings.

"I've never even heard of Suzy Snowflake," I said, fuming when it was suggested by other family members that one of my dolls could be used for Suzy. Why did *I* have to make the sacrifice? Why did Darlene have to *be* the sacrifice?

"Anyone else have any better ideas?" Mother asked.

No one did. Nor did I.

So, against my fervent wishes Darlene not be used at first, I finally acquiesced and allowed her to *pretend* to be Suzy Snowflake. Dressed in a winter coat, hat, scarf, gloves, and red rubber boots, she was to stand in the damp dark cold 'til midnight—eyes opened wide and never blinking, snowflakes piling all around her—while silently throwing up a semi-beauty-queen wave at all the cars filled with Christmas decoration gawkers. These were families, much like mine, who for at least one night during the two weeks of Christmas celebrations, made their rounds from neighborhood to neighborhood, their tires' snow chains nipping rubber while chinking and jangling against the snow-covered asphalt, to view the sights.

"It's okay," I told Darlene, planting her boots in the snow

and pulling her neck scarf tighter to keep her warm. "You're a real trooper. You're only acting as Suzy Snowflake, kind of like a movie star playing a character in a movie. Be brave. Don't be scared. It's only until midnight and then I'll bring you inside and you can sleep with me to warm up before going out again tomorrow. And if anyone tries to kidnap you, scream bloody murder. What don't we do for this family of ours? Talk about a blue Christmas."

I kissed her goodbye and trudged back to the house, miserable at having to leave my best friend out in the freezing weather. Pretending to be a flaky snowflake. I thought about sacrifices. How Jesus was the perfect sacrifice. Surely Darlene and I could get through this without…dying. Christmas was not meant to be blue. People dreamed of white Christmases—white symbolizing purity and kindness. Blue symbolized…sadness.

During the ensuing nights leading up to Christmas, I slept next to the coldest piece of hard plastic ever molded on planet earth. But by morning, Darlene was always ready to take her place back outside next to her Suzy Snowflake sign, never complaining. A perpetual smile on beautiful full lips. Willing and ready to be a sacrificial flake.

A few nights later, most of our extended family had gathered inside our toasty warm home for our big family meal. Besides Darlene, who was doing her duty outside, there was one person missing who sometimes spent Christmas with us. Cousin Charles. Granddaddy's namesake. He'd been making his own sacrifices while fighting in the jungles of Vietnam and had been wounded by friendly fire that left a huge crater in his back. After serving his country, he'd been flown back to Texas and a hospital there while doctors used every skill they had been gifted with to save him.

His sacrifice had been tremendous. His recovery—arduous—and fairly grim early on. Even though we'd exchanged a couple of letters during the war, I'd missed him something fierce back in Tennessee when his letters stopped coming.

He'd been the older cousin who'd set up a Santa's sweat shop in the living room to put together my Barbie Doll Dream House when Santa had dropped it off one year and had forgotten to assemble it. He'd been the cousin to gift me with Barbie's navy blue airline stewardess outfit—my favorite gift that year. And he'd been the cousin who'd pointed out to me one Christmas that Santa had not only made a mistake in bringing me an electric guitar with no amp instead of an acoustic guitar, Santa had also forgotten that Charles couldn't eat chocolates and had left him an entire box—so I wasn't the only one who thought Santa was losing his edge and becoming forgetful.

This blue Christmas evening, we all had Charles on our minds as Uncle Roy said the prayer and blessed the food. Waiting in line to heft ham onto his plate before dipping into the sweet potatoes, Daddy stepped back to look out the picture window. "A car stopped. Looks like the driver has opened his door. Wonder who that could be?"

"Probably someone with car trouble or no snow chains," said Granddaddy.

I ran outside. A redhead with lots of spunk, Darlene was still a doll and couldn't save herself, and no one was running off with my best friend—the gift Santa had brought me when I was in third grade and had asked for a *brunette* three-year-old doll. Darlene and I had made all the sacrifices this Christmas we were going to make. I kept my eyes on the would-be thief who slowly unfolded himself to ease out of the low-slung sports car.

Tall and scarecrow thin, he held onto the car's door to balance himself. He reminded me of someone. But no one I knew acted that ancient and could still drive. When he turned to me and grinned, I knew he wasn't there to kidnap Darlene. But who—

"Surprise! Merry Christmas!"

That voice…that laugh…Charles! Bundled and moving like an old man. Not like the young man who'd left for war, but like someone weary. Battle-worn. With his wound packed and bandaged, he'd been allowed to come home. He'd made it as far as Tennessee to be with extended family for our annual Christmas dinner before trekking home to North Carolina.

While cars hummed past enjoying Christmas decorations, I didn't care who witnessed my joy.

"You're here. I can't believe it! You're really here!" I turned to the pretend Suzy Snowflake. "Darlene! It's Charles!"

"Bet you thought you'd never see *me* again," Charles said, his comment followed by that infectious laugh of his. "What's with the doll?"

Even though he'd been at death's door—a huge chunk of him still missing—he hadn't lost his sarcastic wit. And he'd come home. Not totally whole, but on the mend. Available if Santa forgot to assemble any more presents.

I ran to the house as Daddy and my uncles poured out the front door.

"It's Charles! He's really here!"

The Lord—the real reason we celebrated Christmas to remember His birthday along with His being the sacrificial lamb Who gave all—had answered our prayers and was still performing a healing work in our soldier.

Indeed, the trooper who had sacrificed for all of us had finally made it home. The real trooper—no snowflake. And just in time to help turn my blue Christmas totally white.

Then cousin Charles unwrapped the extra box of chocolates Mother had on hand and already wrapped for someone who might drop in—forgetting he wasn't supposed to eat chocolate because it made his face break out in zits.

And Christmas was somehow Christmas again.

P.S. The rest of the story: Darlene a.k.a. Suzy Snowflake, later had her left index finger bitten off by my youngest child when she was two years old. Even with the loss of her finger, I still dressed Darlene up in an angel costume to stand at the top of the double staircase in the foyer to greet the children's guests who visited during Christmas. Later, I drove from Chattanooga to Nashville with Darlene riding shotgun after my son-in-love's friend, Kevin, heard the stories about Darlene and Chris, my son-in-love, asked me to bring her along to introduce her to Kevin. Once I arrived at Kevin's house for a party, Chris greeted me at my car, then surreptitiously helped Darlene out and upstairs to Kevin's master bathroom where he placed her on the Johnny and left her sitting there all by herself.

About thirty minutes later, Kevin ran down the stairs blubbering about how he'd had the shock of his life seeing someone sitting on his John. Since everyone had burst out laughing, Kevin then wanted to know, "What's Darlene doing in my bathroom? Who put that creepy doll in there? Lovie! Chris! I almost blew Darlene's head off!"

To this day, Chris tells everyone, "Vicki goes everywhere with Darlene riding shotgun so she can drive in the HOV lane (High-occupancy vehicle lane) of the interstate."

And I reply with a laugh, "Chris, you know that is not true. I've only had Darlene riding shotgun a few times. During my moves, and when you invited Darlene to Kevin and Ashley's Christmas party."

~ 4 ~
The Christmas Santa Died and Rudolph Became Toast

When I first had my doubts about there really being a Santa Claus, also wondering why my parents might be outright fat-fibbing to me about the big jolly fat man, I began sleuth-snooping.

It all started when my older siblings let the cat out of the bag after a large rectangular box arrived on our front porch, delivered by the mailman while we were on Christmas break and our parents were busy at work. One of the traitorous siblings—more than likely the one who was seven years older than me, suggested we cut a small hole in the cardboard so we could feel around inside to see what secrets might be tugged out.

Since my hand was tiniest—and probably so my siblings could blame me should anything go wrong and we were found out—it was suggested that my fingers would be the ones to do the surreptitious probing.

When I pulled out a chunky, dark brown hard plastic chair, I realized the box held the dollhouse I'd told Santa about—the same dollhouse that had been on my Santa Claus list—but obviously not the very same dollhouse.

A chunky brown chair? Disgusting.

My siblings laughed.

And all I could think about was that Santa couldn't get anything right—and besides, this was proof he wasn't real.

In all fairness, I'll leave Daddy out of this because Mother did all of the Christmas shopping. Now *she* couldn't even be counted on to pull through for *that* job, and if Mother—smart and always capable—couldn't be depended on to get this Santa business right, how could I depend on God? Was He not real either? If He was real, couldn't He have intervened when Santa… cough…Mother…chose my dollhouse?

Bah humbug! Not only was Santa not real, it was evident that Mother had ordered the dollhouse through a mail order catalog, because the chunky brown chair was the ugliest chair I'd ever seen.

While my siblings laughed at the chair and my bad luck, I gnashed my teeth and inwardly wailed. Though at the time, I couldn't put a name on it because I was only seven, I felt forsaken.

Everything else I touched with my hand through the box's hole was too big to free and would only make the hole much larger if I kept tugging. So, my siblings ordered me to cease and desist. They didn't want to incur *Santa's* wrath or make Mother suspicious that she'd been found out. They wanted to pretend Santa was real for as long as they could for fear some of the presents beneath the tree would be curtailed if it was suspected her little darlings knew the truth.

I kept voting to make the hole larger, however, my siblings—older and more versed in the ways of the world—said absolutely not. "No way are you spoiling Christmas!"

Like—they hadn't already spoiled mine?

All siblings were of the same mind, however; the dollhouse chair was the ugliest brown chair they'd ever laid eyes on.

Ditto! At least we agreed on something. Bah Humbug!

The next two weeks would be a couple of the longest two weeks of my life. And now Christmas was going to be ruined for me. Filled with disappointment, I tried to pretend all was well. I tried to pretend decorating the tree was fun. I tried to enjoy watching the tree's bubble lights but they didn't seem quite as beautiful as they had in previous years and I was only in second grade without too many holidays under my belt that I could recall.

So the sleuth-snooper faked it.

When Daddy put Santa in his sleigh pulled by reindeer on the rooftop—to be all lit up for the Christmas gawkers—and asked me to assist in holding some of the lights for him, I felt like shouting out to my neighborhood friends who were also helping their parents decorate outside, "Hey you guys, it's all a sham—one big huge lie. There is no Fat Man! Santa Claus is a farce! Let me repeat! There is no Santa Claus! Santa is dead, which means Rudolph is toast! And my Mother has the worst taste in the world when it comes to choosing dollhouses!"

But of course, I kept my mouth shut, because if I had outed everyone's parents and convinced the doubters I was right, all of the younger kids in the neighborhood would have been squalling that there was no Santa; therefore no presents from Santa. I'd be the worst kid on the block and my friends would ostracize me forever for spoiling Christmas because their parents would no longer feel pressured to buy their kids presents under the guise of elves working 364 days a year at the North Pole waiting for that one special day.

If all of these new revelations weren't enough trauma for a kid in elementary school, licking the spoon dry of its cake batter when Mother baked a few Christmas cakes wasn't such a treat anymore either. Knowing what I was going to get for Christmas was now a bummer. No surprises in the near future, really, since the dollhouse would be my "big" gift. And worst of all, the dollhouse wasn't even going to be a dainty feminine dollhouse. It was one that was obviously to be decorated with man-cave furniture, and at that tender time I was more of a shabby-chic kind of kid when it came to my dolls and doo-dads. The only conclusion I could wrap my little mind around having to do with all of this travesty was that Mother loved brown. She'd always dressed my sister in brown—which Sis hated—because Mother thought brown dresses accentuated brown eyes.

But I was my own person. I hated brown anything unless it had something to do with chocolate, horses, or dogs. (The color brown later grew on me.)

What in the world was Santa…er…Mother…thinking?

Finally, the climactic morning of the big lie rolled around. I dragged myself out of bed to face what was beneath the tree. Once in the living room, I braced myself to be repulsed by something akin to Fred-Flintstone-digs beneath spruce—at least the tree was real—and fake icicles.

But lo and behold, there in front of me as I rubbed my sleepy eyes, was the most darling dollhouse I'd ever seen. Sure, the ugly chunky brown chair was there, but it was surrounded by the prettiest arranged furniture dressed in blues and pinks that complimented the "wallpaper," and the ugly brown chair that didn't seem so ugly anymore when placed in its darling surroundings.

With a sigh of relief and a new sense of excitement along with jingle bell thrills, I later realized I'd done all of that worrying about being disappointed for nothing. I'd experienced so much doom and gloom leading up to the celebration of the birth of Christ—the real reason for the season—when I could have been rejoicing with gladness all along because I not only had a Savior, I had a pretty cool fake Santa and Rudolf on the rooftop and in the kitchen there were plenty of wooden spoons straight out of cake batter to lick! I didn't have everything I wanted but I had just what I needed—enough.

It wouldn't be until many years later, when I reflected back over my life and my many Jesus moments, that I realized that contemporary people in my lifetime weren't that much different than the ancients of old when it came to God's bailouts and surprises. God always came through at the last minute in olden days so He could teach people to trust Him throughout their life journeys while building faith and hope in Him.

I discovered that God was always there, even during those last minutes when I thought I'd be overrun by chariots and horse hooves before my sea was parted.

And He'll always be there, unless it's my appointed time to be taken home. And then I'll be with Him in the place He's preparing for me.

And when I took a closer look at some of the stories out of the Bible, I realized: When it seemed that Abram wouldn't get the heir he was promised, God stepped in at the last minute during his golden years and blessed him with a son. More than one. When Job's troubles were so horrendous and he thought death might be forthcoming, he was healed and given additional children and renewed wealth to replace what he'd lost. The Red Sea was parted—last minute—when the Israelites thought all was lost. And Jesus cried out from the cross, "My God my God, why have you forsaken me?" The death of Jesus was necessary so mankind could be redeemed through Him.

And even though I couldn't see through the darkness of my so-called man-made hole to discover what else was in store for me in the box dropped off on my front porch of life so many years ago—and I still don't know what my future holds—God has known all along what He has planned for me and He delights in the many gifts He's freely given and still freely gives.

Evidently, God loves delighting His children with surprises though sometimes, in my case, my heart flutters during the delivery buildup.

Even if I never receive another gift from Santa and his elves—or from family members or friends—I've already received the greatest gift of all: Jesus Christ. What a gift He truly is!

And knowing that even if there might be a chunky brown chair in my home in heaven when I get there, because Jesus has promised me a mansion I won't mind. (Don't you just love the KJV—other translations say "rooms" so whatever space I'm in will be perfect.) In fact, I've grown to love the color brown. The same color that enhanced my once dark eyes that have since turned hazel. And I truly feel to this day…super blessed.

~ 5 ~

Sashaying Through Aunt Ruby's Red Door

Some people who have passed on are simply missed 'til it hurts. My Great-Aunt-Ruby is one of these special people. I knew she was great, but I simply called her Aunt Ruby.

My mother was her namesake and loved her Aunt Ruby dearly. When Mother and her younger sister were old enough to travel alone by train, Aunt Ruby and her husband, Uncle Tommy, met the girls at the Chattanooga, Tennessee train station for a weekend of fun. Before the girls left the city for home and the farm, they admired the new clothing they almost always received—Aunt Ruby and Uncle Tommy loved showering the girls with gifts since they didn't yet have a daughter of their own. Mother said the two girls were once gifted with lovely rings, and on the train ride home she held hers up to a sliver of moonlight shining in through the train's window so she could admire her ring all of the way home.

Years later, when I came along, I also enjoyed visiting Aunt Ruby and Uncle Tommy. Now let me fill you in on more about this special Aunt Ruby, the kind and gentle woman I knew: She was one of the first modern-day women to be called "cat woman." All of the strays in the neighborhood, and some not so stray, beat a paw-path to Aunt Ruby's pomegranate red door. The same door that was rounded at the top. A door that—when I think on it—reminds me of something out of a J.R.R. Tolkien book. Aunt Ruby's home was always inviting. And I always enjoyed sashaying through her ruby-red door with its tiny centered window with the door knocker below.

But back to the cats. They meowed their way around, if only to visit cat kin or future cat spouses before Aunt Ruby introduced the females to her veterinarian and sedation and....

I'm ninety-nine percent positive there was a homeless cat hotline and all of the cats in town knew they might get a couple of square meals at Aunt Ruby's house if they underwent a little bit of—let's just call it elective surgery. Either way, they always did receive those square meals. She never turned away a stray, though the males were careful to slink through every now and then on the prowl seeming to know "tomcatting" was an after dark activity—while Aunt Ruby slept and couldn't make a Tom cat, how do I put this delicately, "less than."

When I was in middle school, during the winter months my parents and I visited Aunt Ruby and Uncle Tommy for Friday night suppers. I couldn't wait to get there to watch Uncle Tommy fiddle with his HO trains while I tried to make friends with one of Aunt Ruby's cats. The cat part—never happened. When the red door opened and strangers appeared, the inside cats zoomed through the house for a dark closet somewhere, and the back porch cats flew down the back stairs to the yard and kudzu cover.

Train piddling with Uncle Tommy, however, was always a success. I enjoyed traipsing down to the basement to watch the model trains belt out smoke through their smoke stacks while traveling around the tracks through buildings, across bridges that spanned miniature lakes, and through small towns the creative and gentle man had built at the edge of green forests. The trains and their setup were attached to plywood sheets supported by carpenter's horses so the entire expanse was waist high to Uncle Tommy, making it easier for him to create and play when he wasn't putting together elaborate puzzles, grandfather clocks, or working on other fun projects.

After listening to Uncle Tommy's locomotives sound their whistles for awhile, I'd reluctantly follow him upstairs. Once I reached the tantalizing epicurean smells, I couldn't wait to put my feet beneath Aunt Ruby's table for a spectacular supper. As Mother and Aunt Ruby put last minute touches on the dining table and Daddy and Uncle Tommy chatted in a quiet corner of the living room, I warmed myself by the roaring fire. After being "toasted," I relished the Christmas tree scent and the fragrance of vanilla candles that flickered from the fireplace mantel. Sometimes I thumbed through Aunt Ruby's album collection while singing along with Bing Crosby—"Chestnuts roasting on an open fire...." Oftentimes, I simply curled up with a good read after perusing through the tomes Aunt Ruby's daughter had left behind when she flew the nest. Those books kept me enthralled for hours.

Most enthralling of all, however, was when I threw open Aunt Ruby's French doors to walk out onto her side balcony, feeling like a raven-haired Rapunzel waiting for my prince to call up to me so I would let down my hair.

Most times, all I ever heard was the occasional feral cat squalling in cat speak, "Is this the cat-woman's pad, you know, the woman who serves up all of the chicken and fish meals we've been hearing about? And does she have any more heated beds for strays?" I tuned out cat thoughts and kept pretending to be Rapunzel as Bing kept the carols coming while I waltzed around the outdoor room, dreaming about knights wearing chain mail, carrying jousting lances, and riding black destriers with flowing, silky manes. After the call to the dining room came, I was served fine fare on fancy dishes.

Once, I was amazed that Aunt Ruby had gone an extra mile and creamed the mashed potatoes with a handheld mixer. Not one lump could be found. It was the first time I really understood what being "joyful in all things" meant. I could have been "joyful in all things" with a few lumps because I loved buttery mashed potatoes, but I didn't know how to act with the lump-less spuds. I said, "Even Daddy's mashed potatoes are better than yours, Mother."

Mother laughed about my spud observation and vowed to do better with at-home mashed potatoes in the future. "And no wonder you like your Daddy's mashed potatoes better than mine. He uses an entire stick of butter!" I looked over at Daddy and his ears were wiggling like they always do when he's trying not to laugh. Uncle Tommy couldn't help but let out a chuckle, so Aunt Ruby laughed too.

There was always some type of cake or other delicious dessert for supper at Aunt Ruby's house but when at my house, creative desserts were made only on weekends when Mother had extra time to bake. The surprise for that one special night: Jam Cake. With blackberries. Aunt Ruby knew Daddy loved blackberries.

After supper and dessert, we gathered in the living room before the fire where Christmas visits were incredibly entertaining.

I couldn't wait to see if a cat would dive into the Christmas tree searching for imaginary catnip.

Later, after Uncle Tommy had been laid to rest and Aunt Ruby had lived a full and long life during which she'd saved many cats who'd all become her loving friends, she, too, left this world for a better place. I heard through the cat hot-line that she left $10,000 to her neighbor—also a cat woman—so her beloved pets could be taken care of until they, too, expired.

Though I was sad about my aunt's passing, I had to laugh about the $10,000. It was just like Aunt Ruby—she was so special and generous—to take care of her cats, even in death. If she could have she would have saved the world and every living stray that walked its face. She was that loving and that joyful in all things. One thing I knew: When I passed through Aunt Ruby's front door, I would be soundly kissed and hugged. Love, after sashaying through her ruby-red door was a free gift for all.

Aunt Ruby's Jam Cake

1 C. butter, softened
2 C. white sugar
6 eggs
4 C. flour
2 tsp. baking soda
1 tsp. baking powder
1 tsp. cinnamon
1 tsp. cocoa
1 C. buttermilk
2 C. seedless blackberry jam
1 C. golden raisins
2 C. nuts (pecans or if you prefer, black walnuts)
2 Tbsp. water
Optional (1 tsp. ground cloves, 2 tsp. nutmeg, 1 tsp. salt – Aunt Ruby's recipe doesn't include these)

Mix butter and sugar until fluffy. Add eggs one at a time while mixing until each one is blended in. Sift dry ingredients and mix with butter and sugar. Slowly mix in buttermilk and water. Fold in jam, then raisins, and add nuts last.

Grease and flour a deep cake pan if using one pan. Or grease and flour three 8- or 9-inch round pans. If using a deep pan or Bundt pan, preheat oven to 275° F. and bake for 3 hours. If using three pans, bake at 350° for 1 hour and 5 minutes.

Cool in the pans until cool enough to handle. Invert cakes over wire rack if using three round pans.

Frosting:

3 C. white sugar
1 C. milk
½ C. butter
1 tsp. white Karo syrup
2 C. shredded coconut
1 C. crushed pineapple (drained)
2 C. raisins
1 C. nuts

Cook sugar, milk, butter, and syrup until a soft ball forms when tested in cold water. Add remaining ingredients and beat until the icing reaches spreading stage. Spread on cake.

Or, if you don't like icing, save yourself some trouble and sift confectioner's sugar over the cake for a finished naked cake look.

What I love about this cake is that any jam can be used, depending on your taste buds.

~ 6 ~

Dirty Santa

When Thanksgiving holidays were over at my house, the Christmas trees came out of their boxes along with the many ornaments. Though I loved Christmas, I didn't love decorating for Christmas enough to decorate with more than two trees. I put up a 14' tree in the foyer so it could be a cheery sight from the road and decorated it with silver and gold ornaments and ribbons. Then I scooted the ladder over and used virtually invisible fishing line to hang four gold flying angels—all four staggered—from the center of the chandelier. Loving animated dolls, I placed a couple of them around the Christmas tree in the foyer because their dresses blended in with the tree's ornaments.

Then on to the great room's red and green decorated family tree where the children's school ornaments were hung along with candy canes, red bows, and ornaments I'd bought during my travels. Beneath this tree was the Christmas tree skirt I'd sewn together when the kids were little.

Then on to the barn. No trees lit up down there but I did place a horseshoe wreath with a big red bow on the barn doors because horses needed some Christmas cheer as well since the dogs, rabbits and cats had the pleasure of enjoying the outside house wreaths.

In the midst of doing all of this Christmas decorating, I

still taught a children's Wednesday night Bible class at church and later a ladies Wednesday night Bible class. Of course, my ladies' class thought a Christmas get together was a great idea. And I thought a Christmas party was also a splendid idea because everyone agreed to bring a food dish along with a "Dirty Santa" present to exchange. Since the intercom inside the house was no longer working, I decided to hire a harpist to come and play Christmas music so we would have some form of entertainment. Checking with my violin instructor at Cadek Conservatory of Music at the University of Tennessee at Chattanooga he said, "I know just the harpist you need. She's wonderful and has a beautiful harp."

With my dining room table now beautified with a white tablecloth, I was ready to bring out the china and silver along with the punch bowl. But there was one thing I wasn't sure about: Dirty Santa. I'd never exchanged Dirty Santa gifts. What was this all about? Were these gag gifts? Not necessarily. So I wrapped something pretty and useful.

Once the harpist set up her harp in the dining room and everyone began to arrive, the table was quickly filled with the most delectable dishes. Casseroles galore came in along with veggies, fruits, and desserts. The Christmas music wafting throughout the house from the harp was absolutely divine and I saved a special plate of food for the harpist to eat while my guests were occupied with the Dirty Santa event later.

Later finally arrived and we all congregated in the great room to hear the rules of the Dirty Santa game. We hadn't been given a theme, but we had been told that we were to stick to a price limit. Then numbers beginning with 1, 2, 3, etc…were written down on as many small papers as there were people and when completed, all put into a bowl so everyone could pick out a number. The number that the players got determined a player's turn. Then the player assigned with number "1" started the game by selecting any wrapped gift they wanted and opening it so all gathered could see the gift.

Then it was time for the second player to either steal the opened gift from the first player, or take a gift from the pile of unopened gifts. If the second person decided to open a new gift, the turn went to the next, third player; but if the second player chose to steal a gift from the first player, then the first player got to open a new gift and the turn went to the third person.

As the players continued opening and stealing gifts, the rule was that they could not immediately steal the gift that was stolen from themselves. They had to wait for another turn.

With all of this hilarious stealing back and forth—some of those ladies did not want to let go of the gifts they held—how was the game going to end?

I was told that in the basic version of Christmas gift exchange games, once all the gifts are opened, the very first player gets another chance to steal. If they refuse to steal (This was a ladies church class and here we were all stealing and breaking the eighth commandment ha-ha!—but all in fun.) the game ends, otherwise the game continues and ends when someone refuses to steal a gift. However, it is not uncommon, I was told, to have the game follow another variation where stealing continues until a timer set by the players runs out, at which point the game ends.

Thank the good Lord everybody ended up with the gifts they wanted and they stopped stealing! There was a hilariously good time for all, and all left full as ticks...and I couldn't wait to get the dishwasher loaded so I could get off of my feet and into my comfy bed. But first, were the kids asleep? Check. Had the dogs been fed? Check. The horses? Check. The cats and the rabbit? Check. Did I give the harpist her check? Double check. If only I'd set up a tape recorder to record her wonderful Christmas hymns. What talent!

There's always a next time.

~ 7 ~
No Need to Fear Falling

Atop a ten-foot ladder in my foyer, I'd already located a string of burned out Christmas lights—fixed those—and was now hanging white and gold ornaments close to the top of a Christmas tree, worrying about everything. I chided myself, *You cannot misstep because there's no one to take you to the hospital if you fall. And remember, Mother's demise began when she fell and broke her leg while on a chair changing out a bad light bulb.* To make matters worse, the phone rang. I scrambled down the ladder and sprinted to the kitchen for the phone.

My daughter—a state away at college—was on the line.

"Mom, the dealership repaired my car. But are you sitting down? You're not going to believe the bill."

Even knowing the repair would be costly, I wasn't prepared for what came next. Aghast at the four-figure amount, I said, "Right now, I can't write a check to pay a bill like that. Have you called—" She cut me off, her voice strained. "Yes. No help's coming from that end. I was told to call *you*. Mom, how am I going to get home for Christmas?"

Pacing the floor, I could tell my child was extremely stressed. Now I was stressed to the max as well. "What about your friends? Can you catch a ride home with one of them and we'll get the car issues straightened out after Christmas?"

"Everyone from home has already left campus, and besides, the dealership wants me to pick up my car as soon as possible. They want their money." I could tell she was holding back tears. "Mom, what should I do?"

Here it was Christmas and we were both close to tears. Burned out light bulbs and bills were not what the holiday was supposed to be about. Our thoughts should have been on being joyful and celebrating the birth of our Lord instead of sad and fearful, worrying about how to pay for car repairs; how to maneuver through life that was throwing fast balls at every curve.

The blood rushed to my brain and I could feel a jackhammer starting up in my head. *What I would give right now to crawl back into my mother's womb so I wouldn't have to think about finances and flat tires. And then the nonstop taxes I had to pay to a government rife with waste.* Mother, however, was no longer on this earth and besides, the womb trick would be impossible.

I thought about Daddy at home in bed by now—I so needed a listening ear. *Daddy*! I cried within my heart. *I so need to talk to you*! But I didn't want to upset him with current problems. With prostate cancer, an enlarged heart that had already suffered a heart attack when Mother fell and broke her leg, and having recovered from bladder cancer, he was not a well man. Borrowing money from him was out of the question. As an adult, I'd always had too much pride to ask my parents for a dime. Brought up to be independent, I felt once I was a grown woman, it was my place to look after them and see to their needs. Not the other way around. And he didn't need to know I was hurting. No parent should have to see a child in pain. But sometimes…an understanding father is needed through the rough times.

My credit card flashed through my mind. I hated charging anything and always tried to pay a bill off when the statement came, but it seemed I had no other choice than to use a plastic card. Surely money promised to me would arrive soon. If only other people paid their bills on time.

My trust in God couldn't waver now.

"Mom? Are you there?"

I choked back my fears while pulling out my confident voice. "I'm still here. Don't worry honey. I'll call and give the dealership my credit card. After you get the car back, drive safely. I can't wait to have you home for Christmas. We're going to have fun making Red Velvet Cake. I'm trimming the tree now. Tomorrow night, let me know when you're thirty minutes out and I'll have hot chocolate simmering."

The dealership had stayed open late and after giving them my credit card number and hanging up the phone, the blood-rushing-to-my-head feeling worsened along with the pounding. Continuing to pace the floor, I envisioned grooves forming in the hardwood beneath my feet. Crying out to heaven, I poured out a bucket load of sorrows. Within a few minutes, I felt a total peace wash over me. Calm. The noise in my head—gone. Stillness and peace flowed in. I knew all would work out. Somehow. The Christmas tree beckoned from the foyer for a few last minute touches. No fear of falling now.

As I topped the tree with an angel who would be keeping watch, the phone rang again. My heart felt heavy. Who could be calling this late? Don't tell me. A flat tire? Please God. No more bad news. Looking at my watch, I knew Daddy had already been in bed and asleep for at least an hour. Surely he wasn't having another heart attack or ill with something else because if so, the night would be long since he lived an hour away and the nearest hospital was an hour back. "Please let it be someone else with no problems," I pleaded. "A wrong number would be great."

"Hey." The sleepy sounding voice was indeed Daddy's. The knots in my stomach tightened as my knuckles whitened. Where had my calm and peace gone? He continued, "Are you alright?"

"Yes." I quickly let out my breath. "I'm fine. And you? What are you doing up this hour of the night? You should have been asleep an hour ago."

"I *was* asleep. But woke up because I thought I heard you crying out from the back bedroom. Like you were in distress. You sure you're okay?"

I fought back sobs threatening to explode from my chest. I'd handled my emergency by myself. No need to worry him now. But who had awakened him? How had he heard me crying out?

"Vicki, are you sure you're okay? When I heard you cry out, you sounded like you were in deep trouble."

Could it be that while I was anguished and desperately calling out my daddy's name God had allowed him to supernaturally hear me? It had to be. There was no other explanation. This was too good to keep to myself. And Daddy needed to know he wasn't dreaming or going crazy, he really did hear me calling him.

Through joyful tears, I explained the night's dilemma. Without hesitation Daddy said, "All you have to do is drive to my house and write yourself a check. We have to get Peyton home for Christmas."

"Daddy, I don't want you worrying. The problem has already been taken care of and I'm okay with my decision. I'll be fine. The only reason I'm telling you about it now is because God's watching over us and the true story is just too good to keep to myself. My heavenly Father heard me and contacted my earthly father because He knew I needed to talk with you. I think He wanted your child and your grandchild to know we're not alone—you're our earthly backup if we need one. Isn't it amazing that God would wake you by allowing you to supernaturally hear my cry of desperation?"

"Yeah," Daddy said, wide awake now. "That's amazing alright. But next time, instead of pacing the floor until you make yourself sick, call me little girl."

After hanging up the phone, I walked down the hall and stopped to admire my creativity. The angel was still where I'd placed her atop the tree. After the night's happenings, I wouldn't have been surprised if she'd given me a wink and a smile and jumped off the tree to dance. She didn't. And I turned out the foyer light before retiring to bed. But somewhere close by, I knew my guardian angel was twirling a time or two and grinning like a Cheshire cat with a stash of Christmas catnip.

Lying in bed, I marveled about the earlier incident that for a few minutes turned my world upside down. The outcome wasn't what I'd anticipated. I realized that satan had a plan but God had another plan. God's plan was to let me know He was listening. He's always there. He had everything under control. And He could make sure my prayers were answered by connecting my earthly Father to my needs as well; there was no need to have a fear of falling.

The subject of possible future problems popped into my mind. Car problems were especially dreadful. But if I didn't have problems, there would be no need for God to show Himself by using other people, therefore no amazing stories to share with unbelievers as well as believers. *Was that my thought or God's?* Glad my present ordeal was over, I knew I wouldn't trade my experience since I survived it but I sure dreaded the next moment of chaos because Jesus said, "In this world you will have troubles."

I sighed. "Okay God, I know more drama is waiting around the next bend but could you make the long stretches a little longer before the next curve's train wreck?" God wasn't talking. All was quiet on my spiritual battlefront. Yet I knew my previously tragic Christmas had transformed into an epic Christmas—one full of meaning, joy, and promise. And I knew without being told for the umpteenth time that God meant it when He said, "Don't worry about anything; instead, pray about everything. Tell God what you need, and thank him for all He has done. Then you will experience God's peace, which exceeds anything we can understand. His peace will guard your hearts and minds as you live in Christ Jesus." Like Dorothy's mantra in the Wizard of Oz, "There's no place like home," I repeated my own, "There's no need to fear falling."

Then I said goodnight to all those in heavenly places and turned out the last light knowing the real light would never burn out but always be shining, and one day bulb replacement would be a thing of the past: Merry Christmas to all and to all a good night!

My God will meet all your needs
according to his glorious riches in Christ Jesus.

Philippians 4:19 NIV

~ 8 ~

A Christmas Point of View

In Denver for Christmas celebrations with family, the Red Velvet Cake beckoned from its white cake stand while sides for the ham were well on their way to bubbling perfection in the oven when I rceived a phone call. John "Jack" Koblas, a writer/poet friend, wished me a Merry Christmas and asked what I' been up to. As it turned out, this accomplished writer cared nothing for my talk about attending church that morning to celebrate the upcoming birthday of Jesus. Claiming he was an agnostic, he hadn't prayed since his grandmother died after he'd begged God to heal her when he was a child. A lonely man angry at God was putting it mildly. Jack said, "If you want to keep talking with me you'd better stop talking about that religious stuff."

Horse laughing at his gruff jab, I had to give him credit for past accomplishments. Having written over seventy books, Koblas was a Minnesota historian and authority when it came to Jesse and Frank James and the James-Younger gang's last robbery attempt in Minnesota. He'd been a consultant and script writer for various TV documentaries including History Channel, PBS American Experience, Discovery Channel, as well as independent film companies. His 1950s rock n' roll doo-wop band, The Magpies, had also been inducted into the Minnesota Rock and Country Hall of Fame. His lifetime accomplishments were many.

Of course he had no way of knowing I wasn't impressed with celebrities and rock stars because I knew the true Rock Star and when I finally contained my laughter I said, "Well Jacko, the rocks would cry out if I stopped talking about Jesus, God and what all He's done for me. And if you want to keep talking with *me*, you'll have to keep hearing about it."

By now some are wondering how a conservative Southern Christian writer from the Tennessee portion of the Bible Belt became friends with an agnostic writer from Minneapolis, Minnesota who was steeped in socialism with serious issues when it came to "caps"—what he called capitalists. The answer is simple: Facebook. The internet isn't a total waste of time.

When Jack "friended" me, I checked him out through his "wall" conversations to make sure he was legit and not a slasher. Surely he couldn't have had so many people commenting on updates about the ravages of Parkinson's disease and other health ailments if his claims weren't true. I checked out Jack's books on Amazon to verify he was an author and historian. The man was definitely who he claimed to be—his photos matched book back flaps—though he wrote under the name of John Koblas. He'd also written six books on F. Scott Fitzgerald and Sinclair Lewis. But there was one book that had been made into a documentary that caught my attention—*The Jesse James Northfield Raid: Confessions of the Ninth Man*. As a child I had been intrigued by Jesse James.—I used to watch a TV show about the notorious outlaw. I ordered the book. What I read on page three mesmerized me and I messaged Jack. Listen to our later phone conversation:

"Jack, don't you think it incredible that Bill Stiles, the so-called ninth man who was holding horses for the robbery getaway and escaped, was later trying to avoid the law by ducking into a service at the Union Rescue Mission in Los Angeles only to be convicted by the Holy Spirit?"

Jack gave a grunt, basically unresponsive. Rushing on with my excitement, I ignored Jack's lack of enthusiasm about spiritual matters. "Stiles had the 'soup' or nitroglycerin in his hotel room while trying to scope out his next robbery and when the evangelist, Mel Trotter, asked him to give himself to God, Stiles claimed he didn't believe in God because of the horrible lifestyle he had been forced to live. Then when he tried to stand up to leave, he found he had no control over his legs.

"Let me read what you wrote while quoting him: 'I do not know what you think,' recalled the outlaw, 'but I know my legs were fastened to the floor by a power not of this earth. I kept trying to get up, when a woman came and sat down beside me, and urged me to go up to the altar. I listened to her pleadings for a time and then consented to go, thinking it would do me no harm anyway. What seemed so strange to me was that I did not have any power to resist. It was not the woman, for I had been a woman-hater since my early life; it was the power of God. As soon as I gave my consent my legs were released, and I went up and knelt at the altar.'

"Jack, don't you think that's remarkable—Stiles was so convicted by the Holy Spirit that he wept until he converted to Christianity from a life of hard crime? Didn't this blow you away when you first researched it?"

Jack remained silent about the subject. For the moment.

On the airplane flying home from Denver, I could see the ground below when I heard in my spirit, "Call Jack." Strange.

At this point in our friendship we weren't yet writing together, normally talking about once a week, and I hadn't planned on hearing from him for several days. When he called, we'd then catch up on the writing life, life in general, and exchange our "points of view."

The plane's circling to land. I can't call right now and besides, I'll wait until Thursday for his call.

Then I heard again in my spirit, "Call Jack as soon as you get off the plane."

Detailed this time. There was an urgency to these messages but as usual I was thinking, *Where is this coming from?* Reasoning it had to be from God because the devil would gloat if we all dropped dead and went to hell, I mumbled, "Lord, can't I wait until I find my luggage and get on the road?"

No more messages. Good. I'd wait. Yet while gathering my bags, I had a nagging feeling that something was wrong. But what could I do from Tennessee?

Buckled into the seat of my car, I made the phone call and someone picked up the phone. "Jack?"

No answer. Then a clear click and disconnect.

Now I was worried. Recent snow dumped on Minnesota was serious fluff. Snowdrifts rode deep and sometimes lasted until May. Jack had shared he'd often thought about the Native American Indian custom of dealing with evident death by leaving the tribe for higher ground to die alone. Since he knew his time was short with so many health issues and he couldn't easily make it to higher ground—after ten years of dealing with his disease he often fell backward and sometimes struggled to eat and walk—he'd decided getting lost in a snowdrift might be a viable solution.

Calling back, I received the answering machine message and left mine. "Just calling to check on you to make sure you haven't ambled outside and wandered into a snowdrift. If you're in a snow drift and have your phone with you listening to this message, call me back."

Two minutes later, my phone rang. "I'm ov…overwhelmed."

"Jack?"

"I'm…I'm overwhelmed."

"You're not in a snowdrift are you? What's wrong? Don't make me come up there with a shovel. You need for me to call an ambulance?"

Hearing his sometimes-weak voice always disturbed and left me with a feeling of helplessness so I tried to use humor to cheer him while offering to make phone calls. There were times when Jack had trouble getting himself into bed. His muscles mutinied and refused to cooperate with his mind. His entire body seemed to shut down. Hallucinations were frequent from the twenty medications he managed to swallow. During rough morning times, when he'd been without meds since sleeping through the night before and the Parkinson's ran through his veins like a freight train jumping track, he'd manage to hit the speed dial button. Once our connection had been made, I'd try to coax him through each dilemma. Living in a nursing home was out of the question. He'd decided to tough it out at home alone.

"No, I'm fine."

"You don't sound fine."

"No. I'm not fine. I was having a really bad day. Everything was getting to me. I just needed to talk with you. You always make me laugh. I finally called out and said, 'God, I can't take this anymore. I need to talk with Vicki right now. If there really is a God and you are who you say you are—if you're out there—have her call me. *Now.*' You called within five minutes. I'm...I'm overwhelmed."

Relieved his problem was emotional and spiritual and not extremely physical at the moment, I was delighted God was working in this man's life. "Yes, well while I was on the plane I was being given some orders to call you as soon as I landed. Do you believe God is alive and well now, Jacko?"

Humbled, Jack replied, "He has to be. Or else, how could this happen? This is no coincidence, this has to be of God."

"I think you're right. And he's a God who loves giving gifts."

I couldn't help but laugh with joy. "Merry Christmas Jack."

THE REST OF THE STORY: Believing prayer "works"—I also believe God brings certain people into the paths of others to help us through our travels before we journey home. Before Jack and I met on Facebook, I'd shared with a friend that I was too busy to date anyone but it would be nice to have a guy writer friend to be able to discuss writing—from a man's point of view. Two weeks later, Jack and I were discussing the writing life and soon began a writing project together that has yet to be published. After many more conversations of a spiritual nature and delving into the Bible, I walked Jack through the sinner's prayer. Like Bill Stiles—the outlaw he wrote about—Jack wept with tears pouring down his face. After accepting the Lord Jesus Christ as his Savior, Jack lived three more years, passing into the arms of Jesus in 2013. One day I hope to meet up with him again to enjoy hearing about his latest point of view.

~ 9 ~

The Christmas Tree Skirt

Christmas traditions were always important to me. Not only did I celebrate the Christ child by attending church services, I loved decorating for the holidays.

Many Christmases ago, I longed to sew up a special Christmas skirt for the tree that would stand before the window in my first home's dining room. It was to be a special Christmas tree skirt, not just a white sheet to look like snow, but one that could be passed down in the family, along with Mother's Red Velvet Cake recipe, for many years to come.

With a pattern chosen—can you go wrong with making a basic circle design—I chose fabric for the pie-shaped wedges that would make up the circle of the skirt: Green velvet, red velvet, and a green and red cotton plaid that would be sewn in between the solid green and red velvets. This plaid fabric would also match the large bows that would be wired together for a tree topper with long streamers gracefully hanging down—making my family's tree a traditional red, green, and plaid tree. The tree's ornaments were to be red and green with bubble lights bubbling the same colors. School handmade ornaments could always be added in future years, along with any lovely ornaments I obtained while traveling.

I found a beautiful white lace to sew down the seams to

make the skirt pop and stand out, and then made double layered red bows to be sewn at the bottom of every seam.

I bought more cloth than what was needed so I could make Christmas dresses that matched the Christmas tree skirt—surely I would have a daughter one day.

I bought enough cloth to have one sleeveless dress made from the green velvet. I added pearls on the shoulders along with a white laced strip of trim across the bodice seam. Another dress was made of red velvet, and a third was made of the plaid cloth. A white cotton blouse with a Peter Pan collar would be worn beneath all three dresses, or sometimes, depending on the weather, a warm white turtleneck.

After I had a little girl, a cousin came over to see the drapes I'd made to hang from the ceiling around the baby bed and looked in the nursery's closet. Shirley laughed. "Hey, you have every size in here for her until she gets to high school; but where's the prom dress? She has everything else!" Of course she was exaggerating and being her comedic self, but I confess that when I saw a darling outfit that was really cute—and even better, on sale—I bought it knowing a baby girl would grow into it.

After the dresses were made, I started on the Christmas tree skirt. To quote an old cliché, had I, "bitten off more than I could chew?"

There was no problem assembling and sewing the topper; however, it was lined and that made two layers of fabric to sew through when attaching the lace strips along the seams. Plus, velvet is thicker than cotton plaid and I wasn't prepared for the intense struggle with running all that fabric beneath the foot attachment on my sewing machine.

I had a plan and had spent the money and I would not be defeated. I managed to make the tree skirt like someone would eat an elephant. One bite at a time. When finished, the tree skirt was beautiful. After showing it to some friends, comments were made, "Make me one—that's the prettiest Christmas tree skirt I've ever seen!"

"Not on your life! This is one of the hardest projects I've ever worked on and it had better last a lifetime and another generation's lifetime because I'm never making another one of these skirts—ever again!"

When Thanksgiving rolled around and the turkey had been eaten and all the decorations were put away, out came the Christmas decorations. Up went the balled live spruce tree, and after the tree's limbs were decorated out came the Christmas tree skirt. And that's when I started one of my family's traditions. We each had to try on the Christmas tree skirt, tell the year, our age and if in school, the grade, and then give the skirt a big twirl—all in front of a video camera. Only then would the Christmas tree skirt take its place beneath the tree—ready for colorfully wrapped packages.

When my daughter married and moved to San Francisco, California, I decided it was time the Christmas tree skirt should go with her…along with her English bulldog named Duchess Tula Belle of Oxford, Mississippi, aka "Tootie." Both, when shipped to California, were less for me to deal with. Let the younger folk put up a Christmas tree and host Christmas dinner if they weren't flying home.

Fortunately, from then on the Christmas tree was already assembled and decorated before I arrived to celebrate Christmas so

I didn't have to participate in the skirt twirling anymore. I did buy a beautiful white cake stand for the newlyweds in San Francisco so my child could also make Mother's regal Red Velvet Cake.

One year, I received a video from my daughter and her husband. By this second year of marriage the kids had moved to Denver, Colorado. A guy friend of theirs happened to be visiting them and Tootie when they were putting up their Christmas tree. My son-in-love was reminded by his traditional Southern wife who loves traditions, "Don't forget, we can't put the Christmas tree skirt under the tree unless we try it on and give it a twirl like we did last year. I have to send Mom a video."

Their guest was amused. And curious. "What's all this about twirling a Christmas tree skirt?"

My child filled him in. "Mom started a family tradition years ago when I was little. Each year before the skirt went beneath the tree after the ornaments were hung, we each had to put the skirt on, state the year, our full name, our age, our school grade, and then had to give the skirt a big twirl."

The guest laughed and jumped up. "Hey, I want to participate—I'm next!"

After that second Christmas, the kids headed back to Tennessee where they'd met and where my child grew up. From then on, I once again became a part of the Christmas decoration event and now, there are three little girls trying on that same Christmas tree skirt I made forty years ago. Each one, after stating the year, her full name, and her age, tries to beat her sisters with the biggest skirt twirl.

And I, well I enjoy the skirt twirling from across the room. And doubt that I'll ever get that skirt around my waist in the future, unless I stop eating Red Velvet Cake that my daughter now makes every year to continue her grandmother's Christmas tradition from long ago.

When it comes time for the Christmas tree skirt to be passed down, things will get interesting. Maybe the granddaughter who gets the skirt needs to host the dinner and bake the cake!

~ 10 ~
Counting Southern Treasures Through the First Noel

Dearest Hayden Noelle,

It's nearing Christmas, the time the birth of Jesus Christ our Savior is celebrated, and I can't help but think about how blessed I am to have been brought up in the South—the Bible Belt, Chattanooga, Tennessee being the buckle of that belt—and to know the true meaning of Christmas.

As I'm driving through the gate that leads to your great-grandparents' retirement home on a mountaintop in north Alabama, I remember the story Mother told of my niece, her first grandchild, when they were in the car on their way to town. Before they left the mountain farm the three-year-old jumped from the front seat to the back. Mother thought it strange that like lightning, she'd changed her seating arrangement. But then mother's nose began to twitch and she exclaimed, "Whew-eee! I think I smell a skunk!" The three-year-old held her perky nose and replied, "I know! I smell it too! And I think it's Paw Paw."

That is only one of the many funny family stories I recalled while driving down the road to the homeplace where so many Christmas celebrations were enjoyed after Meco and Paw Paw moved to their farm after leaving their city home.

Smoke now curls high above tall lonesome pines that stand around like soldiers guarding azaleas and roses that will once again bloom pink and white blossoms in spring. Opening the front door of the house with a stone foundation and a green metal roof, I'm now inside with memories flooding in through the foyer. I spot the cedar Christmas tree that always stood majestic in the corner so the lights could be seen through the window by visitors. The star on top shines, projecting a soft light to wayfaring strangers and friends alike. Bubble lights bubble red, green, yellow, and blue, as cedar scent wafts through the cathedral ceilinged great room to mingle with the scent of pine boughs draped from a mantel graced with hoards of competing Santas of all shapes and sizes.

A creche, complete with camels and wise men—magi—bearing gold, frankincense, and myrrh, graces the antique Klondike ice box that once kept another of our log cabin's food cold with chunky blocks of ice, but is now the keeper of crayons, coloring books, and secret little whispery girl things.

The smell of burning logs and hickory wood smoke emanates from the fire, one log tumbling from its high place and breaking in two before the mammoth back log, scattering red hot coals to the front of the deep hearth while sparks fly to be caught by the heavy fire screen guarding the yawning mouth of the cavernous fireplace.

Mother, or Meco as first grandchild dubbed her because she couldn't say grandmother, sits on her end of the sofa with excitement lilting her voice. Listen to her: "Hear the tramping in the fireplace girls? That means a snow is coming. It's time to string cranberries and popcorn for the tree. Who wants to help me make hot chocolate first?"

Down the hallway, I peek into the front bedroom where my toddler daughters slept—one of them is your Mama—when they weren't dreaming of visions of sugar plums dancing in their heads and fussing with each other over…well…just about everything. Mother's voice trills out of the master bedroom. "Paw Paw, go in there and tell your grandchildren to get quiet and go to sleep." And Paw Paw's reply: "Those are your grandchildren, Meco. You go tell them. Mine are in Memphis and that's where I hope they stay." And I can visualize his ears wiggling when he thought he'd made a funny. That's how I knew, when he had his back to me, if he was joking.

When I leave the hallway to step back down into the sunken family room, I hear Christmas packages being unwrapped, the tearing of tissue paper and the popping sound grosgrain ribbon makes when stretched tight to breaking, amidst Daddy's laughter right before he plops a chocolate covered cherry into his mouth and pipes, "Who is the prankster who gave me this rubber chicken?"

A smile covers my entire face and I stay silent, stepping up into the kitchen from the sunken family room, Daddy's left eyebrow raised as he stares suspiciously at me while Bing Crosby croons, "I'm dreaming of a white Christmas," from the ancient stereo's turntable.

It's in the kitchen's bay window where I hear the dessert table groaning from six or seven cakes—Red Velvet Cake queen among them—and at least four meringued pies, as the fried corn and okra stay warm while waiting on the turkey to fry. I count the other vegetable sides with cornbread dressing, broccoli and cheese casserole, and deviled eggs among many more long steaming Pyrex dishes of delights and wonder where the rolls will sit once heated and waiting to be drenched in butter before being washed down with sweet tea.

It's then Mother's voice calls from the family room. "Okay now, I've received two boxes of Chanel Number 5 bath powder. Maybe this will be another four-bottles-of-White-Shoulders-perfume Christmas like what happened one year when we lived in Chattanooga. Who knew I'd actually get what I hinted for this year!" And the fragrance of happiness and joy mingles with the nutmeg scent wafting from squares scored into a hunk of ham glistening from the oven that will feed over thirty hungry mouths.

Walking from the kitchen and into the mud room, I spy Great-Grandmother Shug's (Big Mama) old wood stove standing her ground in the corner, her new resting place once Big Mama had slipped through the veil to be with our Lord. And I can't count the many meals prepared on heavy stove eyes—not only in Big Mama's home but in the log cabin summer home on two hundred acres Meco and Paw Paw once owned at the foot of the mountain in an Alabama cove.

I remember sleeping in fluffy-fat feather beds one of my grandmothers had stitched, listening to mountain lions squall at night in the wooded thickets deep beyond chinked logs and screened windows that kept away mosquitoes and bats, slithery crawlers and creatures, and icky-acky things that go bump in the night.

Stepping out onto the back porch to inhale fresh December air I spot the hummingbird feeders and remember hoards of tiny ruby throated birds flying in and treading summer air with their wings, waiting their turns while sipping from nearby

Rose of Sharon tree blossoms. The trees are transplants from Grandmother and Granddaddy's home place of nine hundred acres of farm and mountain land down the dirt road from our old farm that rested next to theirs.

I sit in Mother's rocker and rock. The cool breeze kissing my face. And I rock some more, reminiscing about Daddy driving a tractor pulling a wagon of hay around the community to bring family and friends to our big bonfire wiener roasts that always guaranteed a marshmallow fight or two. Okay, maybe three to a dozen—when Meco and Paw Paw owned another farm in another sacred place.

It's from this very porch I can see down into the valley of autumnal cotton pickin' sunsets where Mother and Daddy and kindred spirits once trod. I also witness red-tailed hawks soaring and circling on wind currents above the silver ribboned Tennessee River. And from this porch rattlesnakes can sometimes be spotted slithering through tall grass, along with Rocky Raccoon and a possum meandering through the back yard searching for discarded corn cobs and supper leftovers before they hole up somewhere to survive the onslaught of winter.

I once even saw a red fox sneak through. He was headed for the ancient stone chimney near the spring that feeds the pond—all that's left of a great-uncle's and great-aunt's homeplace that was settled early atop this rugged, windswept mountain where stars might be touched if one only believes it can be done from a fairly tall ladder while standing on tippy-toes.

Everyone inside opening Christmas gifts knows that beyond the spectacular and sparkly starwork above them, their guardian angels watch over them and sometimes appear when needed.

The soft lowing of a heifer breaks through my reverie, and I'm reminded of your mother's on-the-spot song writing skills when Paw Paw was out of the truck feeding his cattle. I listen to a four-year-old daughter sing: "If the bully gets my grandfather, I'll run and save his life. I'll run and save his life." That talent must have come from her Scotch-Irish side along with those who originally hailed from England before sailing to Pennsylvania to end up in Tennessee and north Alabama by way of Virginia and then North Carolina Revolutionary War land grants.

I leave the porch overlooking the valley below where my parents and ancestors are buried in a cemetery that overlooks a million footsteps that knew a ton of sorrow and wheelbarrows full of joy. And I recall the many dinners on the ground next to the chapel that Meco helped raise money to restore—now flattened by the devastating tornadoes that uprooted coffins and gravestones alike while ripping ancient oaks from deep moorings to leave gaping holes in the ground.

But then I smile because a photo of Daddy and his kith and kin shows them eating dinner on the ground at the chapel, the inspiration for another beloved story. And I think about you, the latest addition to our family, eight-months-in-the-womb Hayden Noelle—the first *Noelle* or first birth grandchild of mine belonging to your Mom's and Dad's next generation of new beginnings, new memories, and new Christmases.

I'll be back to rock some more on this mountaintop back porch waiting to celebrate the birthday of our Lord and thinking about your arrival while overlooking the paths of my ancestors who have come and gone. I'm counting my Southern treasures as the angels in heaven and guardian angels watching over us rejoice at your coming. And I can't wait to meet you, precious one.

I can't wait to share with you about the very *first* Noel and the true meaning of Christmas—that no matter how many homes and holidays and kith and kin come and go like the tides of the ocean rushing in to rush back out again, you will always have a Savior's birthday to celebrate, a Savior who is steadfast and true. For Jesus says, *"Lo, I am with you alway, even unto the end of the world. Amen."* Matthew 28:20b KJV

With Love,

Lovie

For Your Very First Christmas

~ 11 ~
Trinity's Grace

A week before Christmas, as I held a cup of coffee while pondering the meaning of strange happenings, I greeted my grown daughter with, "This morning, I was looking out of the upstairs bedroom window and I saw an angel on your front lawn."

Peyton's eyes widened. "No. Mom, you didn't." When she realized I wasn't kidding, she dared to say, "Where?"

Concerned about what the sighting might mean—and not realizing how my revelation had come across—I said, "Yes. I did. Smack dab in the middle of your lawn. The angel was lying in the grass. All white. About ten inches long, and about five or six inches wide. Oddly enough, there was a string attached to it."

Peyton looked relieved. It hadn't yet dawned on me that my child might think I was "seeing things." Hallucinating. Losing my marbles. In earnest, I was puzzled. *Omen? Was something odd about to happen? Was I finally going to encounter a real angel?*

I walked to the front door and looked out. Back in the kitchen, I said, "It's gone."

Peyton replied, "Well, the yard guys just left. They must have done something with it."

I shook my head and mumbled, "Uh-hmmmm."

But why did I feel that something out of the ordinary was in the making?

Later, I headed home across Monteagle Mountain. Sometimes on this leg of my journey home, I detoured from the interstate to stop off at Sewanee University. During the holidays beautiful wreaths enhanced the church doors while church bells rang. And the names and dates on the old gravestones in the campus cemetery intrigued me. Whether winter, spring, summer, or fall, the campus was always beautiful. Peaceful. This day, there was low lying fog. Perhaps I wasn't too wise leaving the interstate to drive in the gray-white soup.

An upcoming building distracted me from my musings. On the side of the road stood a small establishment that sold pottery. Or claimed to sell pottery. How many times had I passed the place of business wanting to go inside for a peek? But how many times had the pottery place looked closed to the world? There were never any lights on. And no cars parked outside.

This time, I'd at least pull in and knock on the door on my way back home. For now, I couldn't wait to see how my favorite double doors on the Sewanee campus were decorated. Every year, the wreaths were different. This year was another year I wouldn't be disappointed. Through the mist, the wreaths I spotted were green decorated with holiday ribbon the color of subdued earth tones.

Beautiful.

Grabbing my iPhone, I jumped out of my car to take a quick photo. That's when I heard music. Bells ringing. I hadn't heard the hymn playing in ages. Stopping long enough to snap a picture, I decided to video the wreaths with the music playing in the background. On the way back to the car, I sang what few words I could remember.

> Angels we have heard on high,
> Singing sweetly o'er the plains

Didn't sound right. Maybe I was throwing some "Star Spangled Banner" or "America the Beautiful" in there. But the chorus I could recall.

> Gloria in excelsis Deo.
> Gloria in excelsis Deo.

At least I recalled the chorus. I'd have to look up the verses when I got home. And what did the Latin word *excelsis* mean? Not only was the mountain foggy, my brain was foggy. Surely I'd known every verse at one time while in the junior choir in church. That was a long time ago.

On the way back to the interstate, there it was. The log cabin with the pottery in the window. No lights. No cars. But there was one sign of life. Smoke curled from a chimney, headed for the heavens. Turning the wheel, I parked in front, then saw someone crack the door open. Taking the gesture as a welcome, I opened the door wider. A guy was on the phone and also trying to turn on lights. He smiled and nodded. "Come on in. I'll get these lights on in a minute."

"Don't mind me," I said. "I'll just take a look around while you're finishing your call."

Before I turned around, the cutest little girl, I guessed to be around ten years of age, popped out from behind another door. With blonde hair, a bright smile, and a willingness to help, she said, "Are you looking for something special?"

She pointed out a couple of hand-knitted baby hats. "Need a hat for a baby?" One was blue striped. In the dim light, the other looked orange. *Seriously? Orange for a baby?* Babies usually wore pastel colors. No interest there.

"I'm just browsing to see what I can find. Besides, my granddaughters are three and almost five." Honestly, I'd already bought all of my Christmas presents and had promised myself I was doing nothing more than looking. No more spending. Not one more penny. Celebrating Christmas was always way too expensive. Time to save money. Never knew what the future would bring.

"Those hats definitely wouldn't fit then." The child began pointing out different pieces of pottery. "My mom made these."

Within a few sentences, she shared that her mom was ill with breast cancer. *Christmas. And a child's mother was suffering?* I tried to keep my moans silent and checked my tears. Fought them back. Then couldn't help it—while still browsing—should I ask? "How's your mom doing? Is she better?"

"Mmmm. Not really. The doctors aren't sure if she'll get better. Do you like this bowl? Oh." She took a closer look. "It's a yarn bowl." She pointed out the slit in the side of the bowl where the yarn should be placed to keep from tangling.

"You know, I've been wanting one of those." And I had been. For quite awhile. But for years I'd made do without a yarn bowl while knitting and with yarn bowls being pricey…I did not need a yarn bowl. "What's your Mom's name. I'll be praying for her."

"Shawneeg."

"What an interesting name." I picked up the yarn bowl and gave it a good once over. "I believe I need me a yarn bowl." The child's eyes lit up while a smile covered her face as she directed my attention to more of her mother's pottery. "Are all of these other beautiful mugs and bowls by different potters?"

"Yes," replied the little imp with a laugh. "About eighteen others have their pottery here." With a grin, she motioned me elsewhere. "There's more of Mom's work in this other room."

"Well, let's go see more of her pieces."

The child's father stepped from an adjoining office and apologized again, this time for the cold room. I knew all about trying to be a good steward of God's money. Saving on electric bills had always been a priority. And besides. It wasn't fair this child's mother was deathly ill. During the week of Christmas. *Cancer. Hospital bills. God, how fair is that? She's just a child. She needs her mother. Please heal her mother.*

"You have quite the little salesgirl here. You might want to let her help all of your customers." The child's father grinned before going back to his phone call.

That's when I saw it. That one piece I might not be able to live without. Before me was a light blue bowl. And in the bottom of the bowl was a raised cross of dark blue glass. The cross. *Christmas. The birthday of Jesus who would die on a cross. Times are probably difficult right now with medical expenses.* No. I couldn't afford anything else. I didn't know what other bills might pop up myself. I'd just had two windfall trees removed from my lawn. Health insurance was out the roof. There was always something. Better not buy another thing.

But that bowl could be such an incredible conversation piece. I imagined a party where people scraped the bottom of the shrimp dip bowl to find, lo and behold, a cross at the bottom. *Just a reality check friends. Ha-ha! Heaven or hell—wanted to make sure my guests are sure of their salvation. Does everyone know where they're going? I got a whiff of eau de sulfur when I checked a few of your coats. Relax—just kidding! Here's a cracker. Help yourself to some more dip.* So Shawneeg was a Christian. At least she was a praying woman. She needed a miracle.

The child before me pointed out another piece as I moved away from the bowl with the dark blue cross. "Oh honey, I'd buy every piece in this shop if I could." She giggled. *How could this precious child laugh when her mother was near death?*

"If you had a thousand dollar discount?"

Then *I* began to laugh. And I was shown more Mom pieces. "Mom said this plate has a mistake in it. She never liked these plates because of the mistakes." The child had become wistful, perhaps thinking about her future without her mother, thinking about what might have been. With a voice tender and sweet she added, "But I think they're pretty."

"Mistakes sometimes make the pottery even more special," I replied. "More interesting. Or whimsical." I recalled the time my friend Suzanne and I took a pottery class and I'd thrown a few pieces of pottery on a wheel. I knew about mistakes and how to use those mistakes to make a work of art come alive. And functional. Even educational. I once used a vase with a hole in the bottom to teach a children's class at church that like people, even the imperfect can be used. "I think those plates are pretty too, but I *must* have the bowl with the cross inside. And I think that will do me." I had to make my escape before the child talked me into mortgaging my home to buy out the rest of the store.

"Dad, I think she's ready to check out."

"What's your name?" I asked the blonde beauty while I waited on her father to add up my small haul.

"Trinity Grace."

Caught off guard again, I replied, "That's one of the most beautiful names—ever." If I didn't get out of the store soon, I felt I would burst into tears. Everything about this visit reeked of a God who arranges encounters.

Choking back my emotions, I said, "I'm going to have another granddaughter soon. Her name is Hope."

The angelic child stepped back over to the shelf that held the hand knitted baby hats she'd previously tried to sell me. She handed me the orange looking hat. I said, "Oh no! Don't tell me the hat says Hope on it?" By the sparkle in her eyes I knew I'd guessed at a truth and we both laughed together. And she knew she'd made another sale. Because there at the top of the hat was a wooden button that indeed had the word Hope on it.

"Okay. I have to have it, but is this orange? What color is this, I don't have my glasses on."

If I was buying a baby an orange hat what in the world would go with this color? It would have to be a Big Orange baby Hope. Go Vols. My alma mater.

"It's not orange," said Trinity Grace. "It's red."

Adjusting my glasses, I held the hat up to the light. Oh, my! It had been red all along. "Well, Dad, guess you'll have to ring this sale up as well. Like I said, you need to have your daughter help *all* of your customers. By the way, how's your wife doing. Trinity Grace told me about her cancer."

With measured words, I was told, "We've been to Mayo Clinic recently. That's why we haven't been in the shop lately. The doctors have Shawneeg on medication and she's had treatments but the cancer has gone into her back as well as her brain. We drive to Chattanooga for her treatments now, so it's not as far away."

I assured the man before me that I would pray for her and have others pray for her. Then I asked, "I'm just wondering…it's obvious your wife is a Christian since she put a cross in a bowl before firing it…and I'm wondering if she had an incredible God moment when she came to the Lord? Any special story there?"

"Not really. One thing though, after she'd been working here at Hallelujah Pottery, the owners decided they wanted to move out west. And they made it possible for Shawneeg to take over the business."

The sign outside—Hallelujah Pottery—should have been a dead giveaway these people were Christ followers.

"Well, I would say that's definitely a God moment when you get a business handed to you." With that, Trinity Grace reached up to hug me goodbye. She squeezed out a big smile and said, "Merry Christmas." I hugged her back and made my exit before I broke down in one sobbing mess. As I started my car, Trinity stood in the door and waved—still smiling. Then a fiery dart pierced my imaginary shield. Either Trinity Grace and her father were the biggest con artists selling their wares or they were the truest Christians I'd ever met. Smiling in the face of adversity.

Down the mountain, I prayed, "Lord, none of this is fair. What's happening to that child and her mother, and a father who may soon lose the love of his life—none of it is fair! And right here at Christmas." Sometimes, death shows no mercy.

Then it hit me—the hand-knitted hat I'd just bought. My unborn granddaughter's full name would be Hope Ruby. The hat, in good light, was a deep ruby red. With a wooden button on top that said Hope. Perhaps earlier, the angel lying on the front lawn did have a message for me after all. The day would be memorable. I would not only be singing about angels, I would be meeting a little angel. Trinity Grace.

When I arrived home, I was shocked to find that someone's vehicle, for the second time, had left the road and torn down a huge section of my four-board fence leaving deep ruts in my pasture. More expense. Good thing I didn't buy out Hallelujah Pottery. This would be a costly repair. *Lord, once again, this is not fair. People destroy my property, leave the scene, and never offer to pay restitution or leave a note to say I'm sorry.*

I was quickly reminded, *For now, you have the money to pay for the damage done, food on your table, and a warm roof over your head, and you're in decent health.*

I get it. Don't sweat the small change. No way was I going to let one more setback get me down. My problems were nothing compared to those of the young family I'd just met.

Then I remembered "Gloria in Excelsis Deo"—glory in the highest to God—and Googled the lyrics.

> Angels we have heard on high,
> Singing sweetly through the night,
> And the mountains in reply
> Echoing their brave delight.
> Gloria in excelsis Deo.
> Gloria in excelsis Deo.

I'd been to the mountain that day and heard from angels on

high. I'd met a brave little girl and her father who echoed the joy of angels on a mountaintop they called home—even with death stalking at their door.

> Shepherds, why this jubilee?
> Why these songs of happy cheer?
> What great brightness did you see?
> What glad tiding did you hear?
> Gloria in excelsis Deo.
> Gloria in excelsis Deo.

On the mountaintop, I'd heard a song of happy cheer, seen great brightness in the face of a beautiful child with a name that reassured me that the Father, the Son, and the Holy Spirit were all one and full of grace, no matter the crushing situation. No matter the struggle. No matter the timing. But how could these shepherds I'd just met, these bright angels full of glad tidings, be so jubilant and without even mentioning their faith?

> Come to Bethlehem and see
> Him whose birth the angels sing;
> Come, adore on bended knee
> Christ, the Lord, the new-born King.
> Gloria in excelsis Deo.
> Gloria in excelsis Deo.

How appropo. In only a couple of weeks, I would be traveling to Israel and, if all went well, I would be able to visit Bethlehem.

> See him in a manger laid
> Whom the angels praise above;
> Mary, Joseph, lend your aid,
> While we raise our hearts in love.
> Gloria in excelsis Deo.
> Gloria in excelsis Deo.

And before leaving the mountaintop, through the purchase of a few functional and lovely items, I'd been able to "lend aid" to a father and his child who were also lending aid to God by raising hearts of love to a perfect stranger, therefore raising hearts in love to God even though their own hearts had been saturated with months of mountainous grief.

What to make of all of this heartache and sadness in hearts that were yet still so exquisitely full of joy-filled pain? Trinity was the perfect example of a Christian bestowed with grace and exuding joy even while living in the valley of the shadow of death.

And in all circumstances, God is still here, providing, and still sending angels, though He is highly likely to send angels in human form to help and encourage one another. And through His sovereign Trinity, grace is enough. Experiencing grace is so much better than any thousand-dollar discount.

> And in all things, Gloria in excelsis Deo.
> Hallelujah and Merry Christmas!

Note: Years after meeting Trinity Grace and this story being published in *Merry Christmas Moments*, I was rereading *A Circle of Quiet* by Madeleine L'Engle on March 13, 2023. At the top of page 143 I had written, "Vision—I saw a clay pot and a cross in the pot while reading this." There was no date and I don't recall writing these words, nor do I recall having the vision. So I'm at a loss as to how long it was before God arranged my encounter with Trinity Grace so I could purchase the bowl.

I do recall later dropping the bowl in my kitchen, shattering it. My heart felt as broken as the bowl. At least I still have the yarn bowl to remind me of this beautiful yet heartbreaking encounter.

~ 12 ~

The Big Apple Christmas Prequel

I finally made it to the Big Apple to see the Christmas sights with my daughter Peyton and my son-in-love Chris. And of course all three grandchildren. I'd been to New York City when my kids were smaller so I couldn't wait to make the trip again with grandees. Hayden was seven years old, Harper was now five, and Hope Ruby was not quite two. We'd watched *Home Alone* and *Home Alone 2: Lost in New York* every Christmas so it was time to experience some of what Kevin McCallister experienced when he found himself alone in New York City. Well, maybe not everything, but a taste of enough to help get us in the mood for Christmas when we returned home.

I was told by the grandees that Sven, their Elf on a Shelf would also be making the trip. "But how will Sven be able to go since we're not allowed to touch him?" I asked.

"Mom's putting Sven in a jar," Hayden piped up.

Harper added, "Yeah, Sven's flying too."

I didn't go into the logistics of how Sven was going to get in the jar—perhaps he jumped in during the night while everyone was asleep. Then perhaps when back home and with the jar lid off, he'd magically be swinging from the family room chandelier the next morning. Or better yet, back in Mom's purse she hung over the kitchen desk chair.

One thing I did know, Sven sure had some moves.

After a safe flight we checked into adjoining hotel rooms with our family elf who was placed in the room I slept in with the big girls. Looking out the window, I noticed a huge billboard across the street that advertised the play *Phantom of the Opera*.

"Oh look," I said. *Phantom of the Opera*. I love that play."

"I know, Mom," Peyton said, giving me a traumatized look. "You used to scar me by playing the music from the opera score in the car when you drove me to elementary school. That music nearly scared me to death. Why did you love that play so much?"

"Well, Hayden and Harper," I said, "I guess I traumatized your mother when she was a child. Scarred her for life. I also had a music box I kept in the music room that played the theme song. I suppose that music box scarred her too."

"What was the play about, Lovie?" Hayden asked. "Scar *me!*"

"Are you sure you want to hear about it?"

"Yes!" Her face was full of anticipation. She laughed and once again said, "Scar me, Lovie!"

Harper evidently didn't want to be scarred. She left the room, taking Sven inside his Mason jar to watch TV with Hope in their parents' room.

"Well then Hayden, to hear your mom tell it, the play is about some creepy guy whose face was scarred from a theatre fire. He lived in the bowels of the theatre, way deep underground, and wore a mask to cover half of his face because he'd lost his good looks and felt ashamed to be seen in public. He fell in love with the main star of a play at the theatre where he used to sing and act and now watched her through a two-way mirror."

"Now that is the creepiest *ever*!" Peyton said. "He was trying to kidnap the actress when she was in love with someone else. Why did you love that play so, Mom?"

"I guess I've always felt sorry for the underdogs of this world. And he was so terribly lonely living in the shadows. He'd lost everything. He could no longer be the handsome star. He was out of a job. No woman would want to look at him. He was sad and lonely. Now is that so scary? He was pitiful. I felt sorry for the poor guy. Granted, he shouldn't have been a peeping Tom watching her through the mirror, but the music is beautiful. Haunting."

Peyton served me up an eye-roll.

Hayden seemed as though she was taking our conversation all in, but didn't comment. So next on the agenda was hitting the streets and doing some sightseeing. One of our stops was the Plaza Hotel.

Peyton and I had visited the grand hotel years before but Christmas time was absolutely the best time to be there because Christmas trees were everywhere on the main floor and the Old Dame was definitely sparkling her best as one of New York's finest. The hotel even had an area that had a display of the dove ornaments used in *Home Alone 2: Lost in New York.*

Later, we stopped for family photos in front of the iconic red Christmas balls atop the Midtown Manhattan fountain on Sixth Avenue, across from Radio City Music Hall. Designed by Dallas-based company Venue Arts, the Christmas ornaments are twenty-five feet tall. There is still a photo on my phone of a sweet smiling family, followed by a photo of family cracking crazy faces for fun.

That afternoon, we had tickets to see the play *Frozen* while son-in-love Chris stayed at the hotel with Hope so she could take a nap with Sven.

In the theatre, there happened to be an empty aisle seat next to me. Not far along into the show, a young guy eased into the empty seat and sang every song. He had a decent voice. Must have been a wannabe *Frozen* star. Perhaps he'd been cut from the cast and just wanted to watch his friends perform? What happened next: He was removed by security—evidently he'd gotten in somehow—or perhaps he was employed there in some capacity—saw the empty seat, and got as close as he could to the action from the balcony, so he could sing his heart out. Alas, he was removed, and when I looked over at Harper, I noticed she wasn't paying attention to the play. She looked like a wilted Southern belle who needed a long nap to revive herself. Since the play wasn't nearly as good as the movie and those playing the main parts looked nothing like the movie characters, Peyton and I had lost some of the thrill of attending and eased out early with the girls to make sure we could all rest up before dinner.

Peyton had made us reservations at the popular and eclectic restaurant named Serendipity, featured in the movie *Serendipity* filmed in New York City. Its Christmas decorations were whimsical and fun, the menu was huge, the diners were happy and in the Christmas spirit, and the desserts were off the charts when it came to serving size. Our taste buds were in for a real treat and we all were stuffed to the max. Except for Harper. The child who never passed up dessert had hardly touched her food. She wasn't just wilted from all of the activity, she was running a fever and then chilling, to run a fever once again, according to hand touch.

Outside, while waiting on our Uber ride, we took Hope Ruby out of the stroller, and put Harper in. Though she was wearing a coat, the winter winds were too frigid for someone who was not feeling well.

I happened to be wearing a warm sweater beneath my knit cape so I took off the cape and used it as a blanket to wrap Harper up, then tuck in the sides beneath her to keep her teeth from chattering. She was now onto the "chilling" part of whatever was wrong with her, and I was beginning to feel like a Popsicle myself.

When our driver pulled up, we quickly piled into the SUV and headed out into some of the worst New York City traffic jams I'd ever been in. Cars stood at a standstill, so Chris jumped out of the front of the SUV and began looking for a drugstore. "Meet you back at the hotel!"

However, he found a place to purchase Tylenol and made it back to our vehicle before we even budged a tire's length.

Back in the hotel room, the medication began working and Harper seemed to be feeling better so Peyton and Chris left for a late-night play. Since I shared a room with the bigs, I slept with Harper so I could constantly monitor her. The last check, the fever had risen again—so I changed out cold washcloths to put on her face to bring her fever down while Hayden and Hope slept, Hope in the other room softly snoring in her crib. I barely heard Peyton and Chris tiptoe in from the play, and thinking Harper was better, I never dreamed her fever would spike again during the night. So all night I kept those cold washcloths on her cheeks and neck fighting that fever rather than waking up Peyton who can't run the next day on a no-sleep night. Plus, we didn't need a crying toddler on our hands and that's what we could have had if I'd stumbled into the other room, falling over furniture trying to alert Peyton.

By morning, however, Harper was starving and back to her perky and sassy self, ready for a visit to FAO Schwarz toy store. No more fever. What a relief!

The line outside the store looked like a serpentine river of families waiting to look at toys, toys, and more toys. Plush toys. Loud toys. Animated toys. Musical toys. I was grateful for being able to admire the huge Christmas tree outside while listening to a little entertainment nearby keeping the Christmas shoppers happy until we could finally make it through the store doors.

Since the store had several levels, once we crossed the threshold I stayed with Hope Ruby who was happy to sit in her stroller while being mesmerized by the sight of so many toys and such a large crowd of kids and parents. Watching one employee do magic tricks kept us entertained for a good thirty minutes while the bigs shopped with their parents upstairs. Hopie and I then meandered around, spellbound by all of the baby dolls and soft furry animals. When we met back up with the others, the bigs had what they wanted to purchase in their hands and we finally unglued ourselves from that fascinating store.

The next day, we were off to Central Park's Wollman Rink for hot chocolate and ice skating. Chris and I kept Hope Ruby occupied with a drink and snack while Peyton and the bigs skated around and around and around while falling and giggling, and falling some more before looking like ice skating pros. The ice rink was packed and the girls were framed by New York's skyscraper background for a skyline.

What memories were being made!

As we were leaving to go find the horse-drawn carriages for a riding tour, I heard a little voice yelling, "Let me out! Let me out!" Hope Ruby was struggling while trying to free herself from the stroller's shoulder harness that held her prisoner. She longed to be out walking with the big kids. Not happening! We had to rush on to the next adventure and her little legs couldn't keep up!

One horse carriage wouldn't fit all of us, so Hayden hopped into a purple-trimmed carriage with me. We covered ourselves with a deep purple blanket, and then we were off at an even trot. When the carriages approached a wide space in the path, our carriage driver gave a quick flick of the wrist that held the reins, and our horse picked up the trot a pace for a brisk and brief race. Now abreast of the other carriage, we waved at the rest of our gang, while shouting all in jest, "We're beating you, we're winning the race!"

Our drivers slowed our well taken care of gentle giants so they could tell us about our surroundings. Our driver said, "And over there to the left, is the building where John Lennon of the Beatles lived with Yoko Ono…and over to the right is where Kevin McCallister was scared out of his wits when running from the bad guys in *Home Alone 2*, when he almost bumped into the scary looking homeless lady who was covered in the pigeons she was feeding."

So much to take in!

At the hotel that night, Hayden said, "Lovie, let's close the curtains so we don't have to look at the *Phantom of the Opera* guy."

"Are you scared of the phantom too?" I asked, genuinely surprised. "Guess I've scarred you Hayden. But just remember, you asked for it!" We both giggled as she pulled the curtains together. Tight! No lights from the billboard allowed.

When the fun trip to New York was over and we'd returned home, everyone was ready to put up the Christmas tree and bring out the decorations. There were personalized ornaments on the tree for each year of the girls' lives, along with other ornaments from road trips. There was also hot chocolate waiting for little tummies. The Christmas tree skirt I'd made so many years ago was ready to be tried on, given a twirl, as the girls told the year and their ages—the family tradition I'd started decades earlier.

Later, as we listened to Christmas songs and finished hanging a few ornaments we'd missed, we all agreed that Christmas in New York City was a blast. We were so glad we'd made the trip, braving the crowds at the airport and then again on the streets of the Big Apple. But Christmas at home was still cherished over the hustle and bustle of the big city and hordes of locals and tourists.

All agreed except for Hope Ruby. The Big Apple trip was now a blast from her past. Poor little Hopie was now trying to free herself from her high chair while yelling, "Let me out!"

~ 13 ~
The Buyout

When I was a young girl, Mother allowed me to save her Green Stamps. Spending money in the 1960s through the 1970s was fun using Sperry and Hutchinson's Green Stamps that were sold to retailers who then gave them to their customers as rewards for spending money in their stores. This rewards program was launched in 1896. Even some gas stations gave Green Stamps. The more you spent, the more stamps you earned to stick onto the pages of the gift saver books that were full of spit-activated adhesive—back when putting your saliva on stamps was cool. Green Stamp booklets were given to put the green stamps in and after a lick and a press on the page, stamps could be saved up for a future redemption of something out of the Green Book catalog.

 Once a book was full, I started another book to have the required number of books needed for whatever I wanted from the catalog. Combing through the S&H Green Stamp catalog was a form of entertainment.

 One Christmas, I decided that instead of asking Santa Claus for a certain gift, I'd redeem the Green Stamps I'd been saving for a special pink alarm clock I'd been eyeing in the catalog. That way, I knew Santa wouldn't mess up on that particular request, since he sometimes didn't get my requests right. For instance, Darlene

Remember her? I'd asked for the three-year-old doll and made certain to tell Santa I wanted a brunette. He dropped off a ginger. From then on, I never truly trusted that Santa and his elves would get things right. Perhaps the elves had made too many gingers that year and Santa had said, "Go ahead and put the ginger in my bag since we have too many gingers and not enough brunettes to go around. Vicki will grow to love her." Who knows what Santa and the elves really discuss, but I'm thinking the elves goofed up that year and that's the way Santa handled things. True enough, I did grow to love her. But still, I thought Santa really needed to up his game. Maybe retire some of his elves who couldn't get my Christmas lists filled correctly—perhaps let the younger elf generation take over. (But do elves have kids?)

Back to the Green Stamps. One of the items I recall redeeming with the stamps was that pink alarm clock for my bedroom. I loved that little pink alarm clock. And I was so glad when I finally had enough stamps to redeem it. That meant the pink alarm clock was one less thing on my list that Santa and the elves could goof up.

Years later, the word *redemption* once again came onto my radar. I was familiar with saving and redeeming S&H Green Stamps for coveted items, so imagine my thoughts when I realized at an early age that Jesus Christ had redeemed me.

What? Did Jesus save Green Stamps so He could redeem little ol' me? And from there, I began learning about another kind of redemption. God's redemption of mankind via His One and Only Son. God didn't use a book or two of Green Stamps to redeem me. I learned I was much more worthy than the S&H Green Stamps price for an alarm clock. A person would need thousands and thousands of completed Green Stamp books to redeem a person—even if it could be possible. God had a better way for redeeming the part of His creation He loved dearly and had created in His own image.

At first, He couldn't let out the secret of how He would redeem us and save mankind. At first, in the Old Testament books, He could not let the cat out of the bag. He seemed to tease satan with His plan by having His prophets and others write about a mysterious person who would one day appear. The enemy had to stay in the dark where he operated. Not knowing about this redemption process. The process had to remain a mystery—for if satan knew the entire plan, he would try to thwart the plan entirely so he could possess mankind and stay in control. But God gave clues. From the very beginning.

Genesis 3:15 NIV: *I will put enmity between you and the woman, and between your offspring and hers; he will crush your head, and you will strike his heel.*

Satan now knew he would be playing a game of chess between not only God, but between the woman's offspring. He would be striking mankind's heel. But what about this crushing head business? A crushed head meant death. Which satan couldn't allow. So he would have to play this chess game as though his very existence depended on it. And with every newborn babe, satan would try to either kill them or drag them up to the imaginary line he toed with God so he could pull them over the line to his side and hell.

What the devil didn't know is God had an incredible plan for mankind's redemption. A plan for redeeming the people He'd chosen to show the world how to live, along with the Gentiles who did not yet know Him. He continuously told mankind to "return to me." He was a God of second chances. But the people God had created were like sheep. Stubborn. Never looking up to the light. Always looking down, even though God showed them miracles and wonders through His prophets and through His creation. He gave them His Word so His people would know how they were to live and what they were supposed to do. And before that, He spoke to them through the Urim and Thummin used by David to inquire of the Lord.

When a ruler by the name of King Ahaz was stubborn and refused to inquire of the Lord by asking for a sign as God had instructed him to do, the Lord spoke to him through Isaiah anyway. *Then Isaiah said, "Hear now, you house of David. Is it not enough to try the patience of men? Will you try the patience of my God also? Therefore the Lord himself will give you a sign: The virgin will be with child and will give birth to a son, and will call him Immanuel"* (Isaiah 7:13-14 NIV). King Ahaz would have known the meaning of this prophecy. He knew Immanuel meant "God with us." And Ahaz would have known that Immanuel is identified as the true owner of the land in Isaiah 8:8.

He also would have known that "a virgin with child giving birth to a son" was similar to pagan phraseology used to announce the birth of their "gods." Isaiah was not suggesting that Christ's birth was like the birth of a pagan deity. Rather, He knew that a pagan king like Ahaz would know the significance of the prophecy. And if King Ahaz knew what the prophecy meant, the devil would recognize God's words for what they meant as well.

This word redemption was used in reference to purchasing a slave's freedom. Today, we know the word's application has to do with Christ's dying on the cross to purchase our freedom. Before giving our lives to Christ, we were considered to be in a condition of slavery to all types of sin. God has purchased our freedom and we are no longer in bondage to sin or the curse of the law as outlined in the books of the Old Testament.

Galatians 3:13 KJV tells us Christ redeemed us from the curse of the law by becoming a curse for us—for it is written, *"Cursed is every one that hangeth on a tree...."* By being condemned through our sin, we were eternally separated from God. The price to redeem mankind was Jesus—the One and Only Son of God—being willing to go to the cross for us so He could be the perfect sacrifice, the perfect lamb of God, to save mankind. This was God's checkmate against satan. The "buyout" or redemption had to be kept a mystery so the evil one couldn't thwart the plan. He knew God was going to send a Messiah, but who? When?

Satan thought that by killing the first-born of the Hebrews when they were held in slavery under the Egyptian Pharoah the problem would be solved. God, however, provided a way out through the waters, using the sister of Moses as guard and way maker. When a bright star appeared in the sky alerting the wise men that the prophesied Savior was born, satan wriggled his way into King Herod's insecurities in order to have all of the baby boys aged two and under slaughtered. Joseph, earthly father of baby Jesus, was alerted by angels to take the babe to Egypt.

Imagine satan's surprise and anger when Jesus at last revealed Himself to be God's Son. Satan tempted Jesus by telling Him he would give Him power over the kingdoms of the world if only He would bow down and worship him. Jesus refused. He knew Who He was and that He was sent with purpose—to redeem mankind.

The purchase wouldn't be made with S&H Green Stamps. Mankind would be redeemed by the blood of Jesus shed from upon a cross. Our cost—belief that Jesus is God's One and Only Son sent by God to seal the buyout. Jesus paid the price. He gave His life and sacrificed for all of mankind—those who believe in Him. All who believe in Him are freely given this gift of redemption. We didn't have to buy anything to get a few redemption stamps to purchase our freedom and salvation. Jesus was the One who had to give up something—His blood and His life—to redeem us. Part of God's plan.

Once I had this amazing concept soak deep into my little-child brain, I realized Jesus was the real deal. Didn't matter that we celebrated the birthday of Christ on December 25 because we don't know His real birthday. Didn't matter if we'd sinned—all humans sin; that's why Jesus had to be born as a baby to eventually grow up to preach the good news that we could be saved from our sin if we repented and believed in Him. It was once I grasped the concept of redemption—that it is something other than exchanging stamps for a pink alarm clock—that I could be redeemed, and that I experienced receiving the best Christmas gift ever.

~ 14 ~
An Unforgettable Christmas

A Christmas I'll never forget is the one when there was a package with my name on it beneath the tree. That might have been one of the years Mother surrendered and let us have a spruce tree instead of a less expensive cedar. Spruce, to me, was beautiful. The ornaments could hang on a more horizontal branch and were allowed to sparkle and look their best. Peppermint candy canes could also stand out more on the limbs of a spruce, and the bubble lights even seemed to be happier bubbling away on a spruce. Another plus side was the cleanup process wasn't as painful. Though the scent of cedar was divine, once Christmas was over the prickly cedar needles were hard on tender cuticles when trying to pry loose the brittle pieces of the tree that had fallen into the carpet. Whereas cedar needles bit and nipped at tender hands, spruce needles were an easier cleanup.

But back to my present. My name was on the package but the person who had wrapped it and placed it beneath the tree had not signed his or her "John Hancock." Also, upon opening the name tag, there were instructions: "Do not open until Christmas—feed and water every day."

How in the "Sam Hill" as the old timers used to say (I never figured out who Sam Hill was), was I going to feed and water whatever was in the package? Was it a puppy? It would starve before Christmas, still two weeks away.

Every day, I picked up the package and shook it, hoping to hear something. Anything. A whimper. A bark. A squeal. Hopefully not a growl or a hiss.

Finally Christmas arrived and I was saving the present for last, because by now I was sure as the world turns it was from the sibling who liked to fake die in the snow while pretending he was electrocuted by spotlight wires. At last, with everyone watching with bated breath, I picked up the package and gave it another shake. Nothing. After slowly tearing the paper and ribbon off, I opened the large box to discover what it might hold. Something orange and black. Pulling it out of the box, I determined it was some kind of stuffed animal. With wings. Turning it around to an imaginary drum roll, I discovered it was—a vulture! The room filled with laughter. A vulture? Now why would somebody in their right mind give a young girl a vulture?

I will say this, the always "dying to die" fellow could give imaginative gifts. He was the same kid who, when a little tyke, was given a pair of chicken-head houseshoes by Aunt 'Cille and Uncle Roy. Not wanting to put them on, he'd screamed and fought, while rearing back into Aunt 'Cille's arms trying to escape as if the chicken-head houseshoes were real live poisonous snakes or alligators. "They law," Aunt 'Cille said, "I thought he would have loved those."

Then later, when everyone stopped trying to coax him into wearing his new houseshoes, he sneaked upon those chicken-head shoes still in their box, stuck his hands inside them and said, "Watch 'em fight!" while making the chicken heads battle it out during a well-constructed imaginary scene of the chickens biting the tar out of one another when they weren't head butting.

So it's not hard to figure out why he became the person who would gift a vulture.

I kept that vulture until I left for college. When my parents sold their city home and moved to a mountain home they'd finished building on our farm, the vulture moved with them. Imagine my surprise when I visited them for the first time and found the vulture looking down at me from a guest room closet's shelf, with my softball glove and my stuffed chimpanzee on the shelf next to the vulture, keeping it company.

Fast forward to real live vultures as Christmas was closing in one year. I'd seen them every now and then on the roads dining on road kill. I once saw about twenty below my home, sitting on the pasture fence of my farm. Upstairs, poised to step down to my foyer, I looked out the arched window above the front doors and noticed them. I ran to get my binoculars and yes, they were live vultures—one opening its monster wings as though he needed a good stretch after a huge meal. The wing span looked to be about six feet. He must have been head honcho of the Road Kill Dinner Club.

I couldn't see anything dead on the road so I wondered if these vultures were simply passing through, saw my inviting fence, and thought my farm was just the perfect place to take a break. For some reason, vultures creeped me out. Always waiting for a whiff of the dying. Always waiting for someone or something to die. Was this a bad omen? Was something bad going to happen to me or to someone I loved? Were vultures visiting because I'd switched over from secular children's writing to Christian writing? I knew enough to know that the devil doesn't care about those sitting on a pew bench every Sunday listening to sermons but never venturing off the bench they warmed to actually do something for God's Kingdom. If I switched over to Christian writing, would that put me on the devil's radar? Would God allow him to test me like he was allowed to test Job? I'd had many unfortunate incidents happen since I'd told God I'd write for Him.

That image of those vultures sitting on my fence stayed with me when I sold my farm and moved closer to my grandchildren who lived in Nashville.

After relocating, I chose a new pharmacy for my medications. While waiting in the pickup lane of the drive-through, I noticed that in the woods in front of me, there was a tall dead tree that was a popular perch for vultures. I could always count on at least one vulture using the dead tree as a hang-out spot. Every time I looked at one of those vultures, I felt uneasy and remembered the twenty devilish birds sitting on my farm's pasture fence. But why did the vultures make my skin crawl and creep me out so much?

I knew the world needs vultures to clean up the road kill and carrion. They hold an important position in the hierarchy of the food chain. They help keep disease from spreading by cleaning up decaying carcasses. In the Bible, they are considered unclean. God forbade the Israelites to eat birds of prey (Leviticus 11:13 NIV, Deuteronomy 14:12 NIV). Their job is an ugly one. When the Gibeonites were avenged, seven of Saul's descendants were killed and their bodies left exposed to wind, rain, birds of prey, and wild animals. In 1 Samuel 17:44-46 Goliath and David threatened one another with post-death exposure to wild animals and birds of prey. Vultures are a symbol of dishonor and death.

Vultures—in the New Testament—indicate the coming death

and judgment of those who follow the Antichrist (Matthew 24:28 NIV; Luke 17:37 NIV; Revelation 19:19-21 NIV). An angel will call out to the birds of prey, saying, *"Come, gather together for the great supper of God, so that you may eat the flesh of kings, generals, and mighty men, of horses and their riders, and the flesh of all people, free and slave, small and great"* (Revelation 19:17-18 NIV).

So imagine my absolute horror when I arrived home from retrieving my medications to spy a baker's dozen of vultures atop my roof! *Dear God in heaven—what does this mean? I know these creepy birds need a place to rest every now and then and they like to rest atop high places so they can spot a good daily dinner—but my house? Why didn't they choose my neighbor's house?* All I could think about was that when author Rick Bragg's father was dying, he saw creepy things hovering on the foot of his bed and mentioned them to Rick. When Rick wrote about his dad in *All Over But the Shoutin'* he mentioned this last visit and what seemed to be waiting for his father in the afterlife.

Lord, I thought, *what am I to make of this? Am I about to die? Is the devil trying to take me out because I'm now writing for You and telling about Your wonderful deeds? Or is he simply trying to scare me into no longer writing about You? Is this a cease and desist warning? Either one or either way—and yes, this is creeping me out—I'm not stopping with the writing about the one who brought me to the party. Jesus. The rocks would cry out if I stopped writing about my adventures with my Christ and Savior.*

I knew these vultures were created good along with the rest of the creation and their purpose is a result of our fallen world. But why had they landed atop my house? In my lifetime I'd never seen vultures land on the rooftops of homes! And vultures, in the Bible, carry a negative connotation and the Israelites were forbidden to eat them in the Mosaic law—so what in the world was going on? Proverbs 30:17 NIV states, *"The eye that mocks a father, that scorns obedience to a mother, will be pecked out by the ravens of the valley, will be eaten by the vultures."* We know that when Noah's son Ham mocked his father because he saw him in his tent naked after drinking the wine he'd made from his vineyard, and told his two brothers about it, Noah, upon awakening and discovering what his youngest son had done to him, he cursed Canaan—Ham's son and all of his descendants. *"Cursed be Canaan! The lowest of slaves will he be to his brothers"* (Genesis 9:25 NIV).

Knowing the vultures would be above my head upon entering my home, I had the sickest feeling and a dark cloud seemed to enshroud me so—I kid you not—I combat-parked my car in the garage just in case I needed to make a quick getaway. I was not normally a superstitious person who thought a black cat walking across my path was indicative of something bad happening in the future. I never threw a pinch of salt over my left shoulder to keep the devil away after spilling salt. Never believing in leaving one apple on a tree to keep the devil away, I cared not one whit that I left several apples because I couldn't reach them. I never, for good luck, opened the front and back doors at midnight on New Year's Eve to let the old year blow out. After trying to stay awake in front of the television while waiting to watch the ball drop in New York City on New Year's Eve, I was usually the first person to hit the sheets. I never dreamed of allowing a blast of cold air through the house by leaving the doors open. I will confess to eating black-eyed peas on New Year's Day but that was more tradition than thinking eating a pea with a black eye could bring me good luck.

You, dear reader, are probably wondering what happened after the vultures flew off to find another supper to dine on. I concocted a plan and decided no vulture would be eating my carcass before my allotted time was spent on earth. I recalled Deuteronomy 32:3 KJV: *Because I will publish the name of the LORD* and I tackled the job and got down to my Father's business. I took to heart how many times the book of Psalms said, *Sing praises to the LORD enthroned in Zion* [the hill in Jerusalem above the city of David now being excavated]; *proclaim among the nations what he has done* (Psalm 9:11 NIV).

Psalm 9:13-14 NIV: *O LORD, see how my enemies persecute me! Have mercy and lift me up from the gates of death, that I may declare your praises in the gates of the Daughter of Zion and there rejoice in your salvation.* (Daughter of Zion is a metaphor for God's chosen people who will one day—along with gentiles who have been grafted in by believing and accepting Jesus is their Savior—be the bride of Christ talked about in the New Testament.)

Psalm 51:15 NIV: *O Lord open my lips, and my mouth will declare your praise.*

Psalm 18:49 NIV: *I will praise you among the nations, O LORD; I will sing praises to your name.*

Romans 15:9 NIV: *...as it is written: "Therefore I will praise you among the gentiles; I will sing hymns to your name."*

2 Samuel 22:50 NIV: *I will praise you among the nations; I will sing your praises to your name.*

Psalm 105:1-2 NIV: *Give thanks to the LORD, call on his name; make known among the nations what he has done. Sing to him, sing praise to him; tell of all of his wonderful acts.*

Psalm 145:4-6 NIV: *One generation will commend your works to another; they will tell of your mighty acts. They will speak of the glorious splendor of your majesty, and I will meditate on your wonderful works. They will tell of the power of your awesome works, and I will proclaim your great deeds.*

Numerous verses of Scripture tell us to proclaim the name of the Lord. When God made Himself known to Moses via the burning bush, *Then Moses said, "Now show me your glory." And the LORD said, "I will cause all my goodness to pass in front of you. And I will proclaim my name, the LORD, in your presence. I will have mercy on whom I will have mercy, and I will have compassion on whom I will have compassion"* (Exodus 33:18-19 NIV).

Then the LORD came down in the cloud and stood there with him and proclaimed His name, the LORD. And He passed in front of Moses, proclaiming, "The LORD, the LORD, the compassionate and gracious God, slow to anger, abounding in love and faithfulness, maintaining love to thousands, and forgiving wickedness, rebellion and sin. Yet he does not leave the guilty unpunished; he punishes their children for the sin of the fathers to the third and fourth generation. (Exodus 34:5-7 NIV) Later, in Ezekiel 18, we read that a child is not punished for his father's sins. The person who sins will die.

After studying all of these verses, I was further encouraged and motivated to get busy doing the Father's work by writing and telling others about the love of the Father along with His faithfulness. No doubt there will be punishment for sins and a judgment day. The Bible is one big book of many books combined that has the theme of love, repentance, return to me, forgiveness, and saving grace. No doubt God punishes sin. But no doubt God is still a loving God.

That vulture I received as a Christmas gift years ago from a mischievous sibling was certainly an odd present. Who knows what happened to the old orange and black bird. I can't recall. What I can recall is that now Christians are in a stage of gaining more knowledge via the worldwide web. There are those online who would trick us into believing the Bible isn't truth. They are vultures themselves. They like to play "Gotcha" and say that Christmas—December 25—is not the real birthday of Christ. Those who know that lambs were born in the spring near Bethlehem—and that would have possibly been when Jesus would have been born, not December—also know that the twenty-fifth of December was a pagan holiday and the Catholic church blended Christ's birthday with a pagan holiday because the true date of Christ's birth is unknown.

Santa Claus was then added into the mix of celebrations after Saint Nicholas, a 4th-century Greek Christian bishop of Myra (now Demre) in the region of Lycia in the Roman Empire—today's Turkey—gave gifts to the poor.

Then came Father Christmas when England no longer kept the feast day of Saint Nicholas on December 6. The Christmas celebration was moved to December 25 to coincide with Christmas Day. Different countries had a different Father Christmas and the concoction of "the Christmas man" who brought good cheer and gifts eventually helped turn stagnant economies into a bustling time of the year when people left home to "get into the Christmas spirit" by shopping for the perfect gifts for loved ones. Was the person or persons who invented Santa Claus a greedy vulture, or merely trying to help out the economy? These types of vultures do not give you the entire truth. Like the devil, they twist the words of God so they can confuse and devour.

Don't think I'm knocking Christmas or am against all of the gift buying. I love Christmas. The month-long build up to the special day is fun, the food is scrumptious, the choirs exclaiming Gloria in Excelsis Deo are inspired by heaven, and the actual day we celebrate the birth of Christ is my favorite holiday...as long as the real reason for the season is eventually taught to older children that Santa drops off special gifts on Christmas Eve (if you choose to do this for your children for fun), but Jesus is worshipped and praised the next day while celebrating His birth. And that His gift is the most special gift of all, and it's free. Salvation and acceptance into God's family doesn't cost us one single penny.

This gift from God can't be bought, and it's available to rich and poor alike. The Christ gift is that there was the One and only Son of God who died on a cross—the most excruciating death the Romans could think up—shedding His blood and copious tears so that sinful mankind could be saved. And no vultures out there—true birds of prey or truly evil men and women out to destroy mankind because they've had a walk with satan and his demons on the dark side—can ever keep that free gift from those who choose to follow Christ.

When our allotted time on earth is done, vultures might come to strip our carcasses of our flesh if we're not quickly buried, but there is one thing they can never strip us of—the love of Christ and eternal life.

But how does one go about proclaiming the name of the Lord? Testimonies. Sharing with others the Gospel, called the Good News, along with sharing personal testimonies of how God has made Himself known in our own lives. Haven't experienced any personal encounters with God, Jesus, or His Holy Spirit? Ask God what can be done for Him. Ask for wisdom—He promises to give it. Ask to know Him better so a deeper relationship can be formed, and mean it. He won't disappoint. Even if you spot a vulture or two during a lifelong walk with Christ, always know He didn't create man or woman for wrath. We know the ending—He's already told us that we are saved to live eternally with Him in heaven. Jesus has already prepared a place for us there.

Since I'm a writer, I leave one of my books when traveling to help proclaim the name of the Lord—the fruit of my labor for Him. He's given me the Godcident encounters and established my walk; I only write them down as a gift back to Him and others via storytelling. God will then make sure the books I leave get into the hands of those who need them. One who is seeking. Or one who is simply curious and might later delve into God's Word for truth. Perhaps one of my books will lead someone to read further and open up a Bible to study inductively—the best way.

My daughter also leaves books for me when she's traveling. She recently left a book in London for her room maid and another book in Italy. Matthew 9:37-38 NIV states: *Then he said to his disciples, "The harvest is plentiful, but the workers are few. Ask the Lord of the harvest, therefore, to send out workers into his harvest field."*

Just think, the disciples were praying way back then about future Christians and asking for Jesus to send out workers. Those prayers have been kept in a bowl up in heaven (Revelation 5:8) and the promises from those prayers have reached down through the last two thousand years—since Jesus left us—so the Holy Spirit could indwell us and so that we, too, will continue to pray.

As of the publication date of this book, many more are coming to Christ. Christ is appearing to Muslims in Iran and the Middle East and elsewhere. Jesus is still working to save the lost. There are many testimonies online from Jewish people who have come to Christ. Go to oneforisrael.org and click on "Go deeper" to find and read testimonies of Messianic Jews under the "I Met Messiah" videos. Amazing things are happening.

"So what can I do with limited means?" one might ask. Can't afford to give Bibles to those who don't have them? No longer attend church to be with others and help out because of health issues? Can no longer afford to take food into the church's pantry to feed the hungry? There's still plenty of work for willing laborers. Prayers cost nothing. And prayers are powerful and can be prayed morning, noon and night. Anywhere, anytime.

God still uses the hands and feet of people to do His work in the world. Don't be fearful of the vultures who may appear. God made the vultures. God can control the vultures. Don't let the vultures frighten you or be worrisome. Dwell on the reason for the Christmas season.

I'll not only continue to celebrate Christ's birthday, I'll continue to proclaim and publish His name and His works.

May your Christmas be merry and bright, and to all a pleasant sleep and good night!

~ 15 ~
Snowing the Christmas Village

Family traditions are so much fun to make. During the month of December, my family and I partake in some fun events. One year we took the children with friends on a train ride where Santa and Mrs. Claus showed up with a few elves.

We've embarked on a magical journey to see Nashville's Nutcracker performance to also see the splendor of the Sugar Plum Fairy's kingdom while a few mice battled for victory.

Last year, we watched *Home Alone* with the Nashville Symphony playing the movie's songs in real time in Nashville's Schermerhorn Symphony Center.

Christmastime at my house is the night my family comes over for supper, snowing the Charles Dickens' Village assembled on the baby grand piano, opening gifts, and then settling down for a Christmas movie.

Before the precious ones arrive, I've decorated for Christmas inside and out, cleaned the house, cooked, baked, purchased, wrapped, and listened to Christmas music to set the mood, and thought of loved ones long gone who used to make Christmas so special for me.

When the doorbell rings, I open the door to grab

grandchildren for kisses and bear hugs—a ritual Grandmother and Granny always performed when I showed up at their homes.

Once inside, the kids run to the front room to check out their presents beneath the tree. They also check out the Christmas decorations, some stained glass angel ornaments and others handmade for them by me. (It's always nice to have a friend who can teach one how to cut and solder stained glass ornaments that are so original and beautiful—thank you Kathy!)

And then everyone takes a look at the heavy hors d'Oeuvres in the kitchen to sample a few before I round the kids up to make our Christmas punch in the Fitz and Floyd punch bowl set I bought many years ago. The large bowl looks similar to a Santa Claus sack used to hold toys to drop off on Christmas Eve. A creamy white, there is a red cord around the top of the "sack." The cups look like a smaller version of the bowl.

I retrieve a large, cold bottle of ginger ale and a can of frozen fruit mix from the freezer and also a premade Bundt pan ice ring of lemon and lime slices, maraschino cherries, and mandarin orange slices frozen solid in ginger ale.

Then we take a vote on whose turn it is to make the punch. "You emptied the red frozen stuff in the punch bowl last year! Where's the step stool so I can see?"

"Well, you added the fruit ring last year so it's my turn!"

"And it's *my* turn to pour in the ginger ale. So scoot over—I need more room to stir!"

Once the Christmas punch is made and everyone has ladled out their own punch—time to eat! One of the girls blesses our food and gives thanks.

At last it's time for dessert. I've already arranged special

Christmas cookies from Puffy Muffin—one of our favorite places to eat in Brentwood, Tennessee. They make the most beautiful cookies and I've arranged them on a three-tiered plate stand. I also include chocolate covered cherries on one of the plates because those were Daddy's favorite Christmas candies and sharing those goodies are a special way to remember his Christmas tradition when we're celebrating the holidays together. We'll have Mother's and Grandmother's memories with us on Christmas Day when eating Mother's Red Velvet Cake recipe and Grandmother's sage dressing recipe I've made using her dressing pan.

As for other relatives looking down from heaven—you should have started a Christmas tradition so we could include it! But hey, we're still thinking about you all and remembering the fun times!

Cousin Gwen's memory is always in the room because she crocheted me several snowflakes that she then starched for Christmas decorations. I place those on the mantel, hanging from greenery. And of course my treasured friend Suzanne is with us in spirit since she can't travel to be with us while we're enjoying the scent of her Frazier Fir Pine Needle Holiday Candle and munching on the gigantic Danish pastry she's sent through the mail.

Once dessert is finished, it's on to the music room to snow the Charles Dickens' Village. The Ghost from Christmas past used to be a scary character for the girls and they closed the door to the music room if they needed to walk down the hallway. Now, they just make sure to give him a heavy snow dusting after moving him around some while my daughter plays Christmas carols on the piano and my son-in-love helps with "the snowing."

The iced-over pond where the adults and children skate and sled gets a lot of "snow attention," and the fox in the lead ahead of the huntsmen on horses has had so much snow attention his tail has broken off.

Once the village has been snowed, the time has come for the Christmas present reveal. I always have a pile of presents beneath the tree for each child who has their own Christmas paper pattern so they know which presents are theirs without having to check every name tag. With the presents moved to the living room and a plastic garbage bag handy, the fun begins! Tied ribbons are popping and paper is flying around the room, and finally it's time to stuff the garbage in the bag to at last settle down to watch a Christmas movie before the fireplace. By the time the movie is over, it's time for bed.

"Thank you Lovie!"

"Thank you Lovie!"

"Thank you Lovie!"

And out the door they boot-scoot with their gifts and boxes of left over cookies, bundled up for the ride home.

Another Christmas at Lovie's has come and gone. Yet, another Christmas meal will soon come to be shared with extended family and friends who can't make it home for Christmas Eve or Christmas Day. This time there will be more good traditional food and presents, but the main focus will be about the day we celebrate the birthday of Christ.

And I can't wait!

For unto us a child is born, unto us a Son is given: and the government shall be upon his shoulder: and his name shall be called Wonderful, Counsellor, The mighty God, The everlasting Father, The Prince of Peace. Of the increase of his government and peace there shall be no end, upon the throne of David, and upon his kingdom, to order it, and to stablish it with judgment and with justice from henceforth even for ever. The zeal of the Lord of hosts will perform this.

Isaiah 9:6-7 KJV

- 16 -

Sven and the Tornado

Right before Christmas one year, Peyton and Chris flew to Arizona to visit friends who were hosting a party to raise money for a charity, so the grandees and I were at their home with their sheepadoodle dog Bear, and Sven, their Elf on a Shelf who was back in town and full of himself swinging off the chandeliers, hanging out in the fridge eating up all of the cold cuts and desserts, and sometimes hiding out in the most peculiar places—once to be found at the very top of the Christmas tree trying to be the star of the show.

I said to the grandees, "Let's ride around the neighborhood looking at all of the Christmas decorations—want to?" Everyone was all in. By now Hope Ruby was five and knew to call Bear's teeth "sharp" teeth instead of "creepy" teeth when he became rambunctious with her.

As we drove around the streets seeing who had the best Christmas decorations and oohing and aahing over the lights, I heard statements like, "I like that Santa—he's the best!" And "Look at that whopper snowman! He's huuuugggge." And "Those red and green and blue lights are prettier than the all white lights!"

As we drove onto another street, I said, "Look girls! Aren't those pretty wreaths?"

Hayden burst out laughing, "Lovie, you need glasses. Those are bicycle tires…."

Harper chimed in, "And hanging up in the garage!"

The kids all howled about the bicycle tire wreaths and even Hope thought that was a funny.

Before long though, our laughter was over.

"Buuuuuu-tter," said Hope Ruby.

Harper said, "Lovie, Hope won't stop saying butter. Make her stop."

"Why are you two fighting back there?"

"Yeah Hope—stop it!" said Hayden.

"Buuuuuuut-ter. Butter."

"Girl's, what's wrong with her saying butter? I like butter."

"She's so annoying Lovie. She just says it over and over again—something she's heard on TV. Make her stoppppp!"

So I said, "Buuuuuut-ter. I love butter. Hope Ruby, you can say butter all you want. Let's all say buuuuuut-ter!"

We all said "butter" for a hot minute and then the hotness was over. "Listen to the radio girls, there's a tornado watch out for tonight. We have to stay on our toes. Let's pray it passes over and fizzles out before it can do any damage."

Back at the house, we all slipped into our jammies and got into the guest room's king size bed and I told "Lovie" stories until I heard my phone ping a notification. A box had just been delivered and was sitting on my front porch.

"Oh no! My shrimp bundles have just been delivered and I'm not there to put them in the freezer! Everybody up! And let's go. We have to run to my house to save the shrimp bundles and some more items I ordered or there won't be Christmas supper at my house this year."

"Are you kidding?" asked Hayden.

"I'm not going," said Harper.

"Wake up Hope Ruby," I said. "We all have to go—I can't leave you home alone."

"What?"

"Nooooooo!"

Slipping my clothes over my jammies I said, "You can stay in your jammies but everyone out of the bed, now! Let's go save the shrimp bundles!"

We made it down to the subdivision entrance where I stopped. Absolutely no traffic at 9:30 P.M. I said, "This is eerie. No traffic. The sky looks funny." I rolled my window down. "No sounds at all. It feels like what a tornado feels like before it…I forgot! Tornado warnings for tonight. Don't worry. We'll beat it. Seven minutes to my house. Throw the shrimp bundles and other items into the freezer, seven minutes back. You three can stay in the car with the heater running. Shouldn't take me more than four minutes to fill the freezer."

Driving to my house, not a single soul was on the highway. Pulling into my driveway, there sat the shipment of shrimp bundles. No way was I going to let those shrimp bundles end up in Cullman, Alabama or the Gulf if the tornado did indeed touch down. If my home took a direct hit, at least the shrimp bundles would be intact in the freezer. Maybe. I checked the weather radar. The red blob was slowly making its way east of Memphis. It would take hours for the storm to hit the Nashville area. Not today satan. You're not ruining my Christmas supper.

Back at the kids' house, I gave some orders. "Let's put

comforters, pillows, a flashlight, and blankets in your parents' closet—just in case. Then we'll be ready for the worst. Usually these bad storms pass over but I'd rather be as safe as we can get instead of sorry. Then let's get some sleep."

Sleep was wishful thinking.

At one point, I overheard Harper whispering to Hayden in a conspiratorial voice, "Mom and Dad aren't here and if Sven doesn't move tonight then we know none of this is real."

Sven? Oh yeah. The Elf on a shelf who went with us to the Big Apple in a Mason jar. Dude.

Not on my watch were they going to be disappointed in Sven's ability to be a mischievous actor. Nor were we losing shrimp bundles flying to the Land of Oz on my watch. I could just picture shrimp bundles hanging off of trees all over Nashville. Then I remembered the woman in Ringgold, Georgia a few years earlier who decided it would be a good idea to bathe in her tub in the middle of a tornado. Her tub, with her in it, ended up in the Ringgold Taco Bell parking lot. "Dear Lord, it's too late to reorder those shrimp bundles again. Help a girl out here! Let this storm pass. Storm, be still!"

By three A.M. my phone was blaring out a storm warning. Checking radar, I discovered there was more red tinged with pink. Pink meant tornado.

"What is that noise?" asked Harper, her head raised from beneath the covers.

"The tornado warning," Hayden belted out.

"Wake up Hope and let's hit the mattresses girls!"

Once inside the closet with Bear, Hope Ruby said, "Oh no! Sven! What about Sven?" Her eyes looked like coffee cup saucers.

"We can't leave Sven out there! Where is he? Did anyone see Sven?"

I said, "Hopie, Sven can fend for himself. He'll be fine. He knows how to take care of himself. Girls, start singing 'Jesus Loves Me This I Know' while I run out to try and find the flashlight! And no matter what happens, Do Not Open This Closet Door! I'll be right back. Gotta check on the back door real quick too! Under no circumstances do you leave this closet. Do *Not* leave this closet!"

In the family room, I could hear the wind outside whipping tree branches around to quarrel with other trees nearby. The storm was definitely coming. I hated that noise. I'd been in five bonafide tornadoes before, and the sounds those storms made were terrifying once they were near. They sounded like a freight train sounding its horn as it blew through.

Back in the closet I said, "I forgot. The flashlight was already in here with us. I'm cutting the overhead light now. Let's pray girls. Lord, please let this storm pass over us and lose strength. Protect us, our homes and our neighborhoods, and all in this storm's path. Can I get an amen girls?"

They all three cried out in unison, "Amen!"

"How's Bear doing girls?"

I turned on the flashlight and shined it toward Hayden.

"He's good, Lovie," Hayden said, her arms wrapped around him as she shared his bed. He never whimpered. Nor did Hayden. Bear was just glad we were all taking shelter in the closet with him.

"Lovie!" Hope said. "Did you see Sven when you went out?"

"I didn't spot Sven, Hopie. He must have moved during the night to a new place. He wasn't in his same spot so he probably moved to a safer location. Elves have an uncanny way of protecting themselves. Sven will be fine. Let's sing, 'This Little Light of Mine, I'm gonna let it shine...'"

The three grandees chimed in as if they could scare the tornado into taking a time out as they sang their little hearts out.

"'Hide it under a bushel, *No*! I'm gonna let it shine. Let it shine, let it shine, all the time. Don't let satan (whoosh blowing sounds from all of us) it out. I'm gonna let it shine...'"

"Girls, sounds like the worst part is right over us now, keep singing! Dear God, dear God...protect us Jeeeeee-sus!"

"'...let it shine, let it shine, all the time!'"

"Lovie," said Harper in a quiet solemn voice, "I'm...I'm only eight...and...I..."

I shined the flashlight her way and lit up her petrified face. "And you have lots more living to do Harper—keep singing! You will make it to 100 to tell about this night. We're going to be okay. Lord, let this storm pass over us. Protect us and keep us in your loving arms dear Jesus! And Jesus, next year, I'm ordering those shrimp bundles in November! Keep my house safe from this storm so we can have our planned Christmas supper at my house this year. Let this storm pass over Nashville!"

I shined the light on Hope's face. She was almost ready to make a run for the door to check on Sven.

"Hope Ruby! Stay put!" I could feel my face heat up which meant my blood pressure was rising as my heart raced.

"We have to find Sven and bring him into the closet so the storm—"

I cut her off. "Get back into this closet and shut the door *Now*! He's an E*lf*! We can't touch him! Sven is O*n* H*is* O*wn*!"

White lie, white lie, white lie. An elf has made a sinner out of me. Dear God, please do not let that lightning strike me dead!

After a few intense moments of silence I said, "Listen! Girls, I think the worst part of the storm has passed over the house. Where's my phone? I need to check the radar."

Hayden said, "Here it is, Lovie."

"Look girls. Yesssss! The storm has passed. Thank you Jeeeee-sussssss! I think we can get out of this closet now." The girls opened the door and ran out while I rested on the blankets. Worn slap, dab, out. All I could say was, "Thank you Jesus, thank you Jesus, thank you Jesus."

Hope Ruby ran back into the bedroom with both hands over her heart yelling, "*Lovie! Lovie! Lovieeee!*"

What now God—has this precious child had a heart attack? Oh geez! Am I going to have to drive to the emergency room? I am exhausted! I slid across the hardwood floor to find Hope.

"What is it now, Baby? What's wrong, Hopie! Are you okay? Tell me! What's wrong honey?"

"*Lovie! Sven Made It!*"

All I could say to myself was *big woot.*

"*And He Moved Already. He's On Top Of The Mantel!*"

I breathed a heavy sigh of relief. Put my hand over my heart to keep it from flopping out of my chest. Then said, "How do you think that happened, Hope Ruby?"

With a huge grin on her face, she said, "It's maaaaaaagggggic Lovie!"

I can't decide if the grandees are keeping me young or aging me. And big update: The company I ordered shrimp bundles from no longer offers them in their mail order catalog. That could be a plus. I'm tired of chasing after shrimp bundles.

One thing I do know, my family and I will be spending eternity in heaven should a tornado blow us away.

In the meantime, good stories must have conflict. And Sven, well, Sven, tornadoes, and bicycle wreaths along with the word "butter" help provide that conflict. So I suppose Middle Tennessee is the right place to be for this writer and grandmother—for now.

Until the next bit of Christmas drama and a good bit of conflict—*buuuuuuut-ter*! Woot-woot!

~ 17 ~
Red Velvet Cake

Christmas is simply the best holiday of the year. The day the birthday of Christ has been celebrated for centuries. Of course there's gift giving, after all, Jesus received gifts from the Three Wise Men. For a birthday party there must be gifts. And of course Santa somehow worked his way into the holiday since we can't physically give Jesus a gift, other than ourselves—so we give gifts to friends, family, and those who might be in need.

I know I simplified all that some. I like to say, however, that since God, Jesus, and the Holy Spirit are the Trinity living inside of me, of course we can *all* receive Christmas gifts!

And without revealing too much, someone just had to make up a lot of stuff to make life interesting and fun when it comes to "naughty and nice" and "you'd better watch out!" *Wink*

Before the big day, there's the hustle and bustle of buying presents for loved ones and then choosing an angel off the tree at church so we can shop and wrap gifts for local children so they can also have a fun time on Christmas morning after worrying about being spied on and "watched" all year long. "Santa's watching you!"

One of my best Christmas celebrations was when I asked my grandparents for Bibles. I wanted Granny to give me a Bible I had my heart set on for an everyday Bible I needed for Bible class at school, then I wanted my maternal grandparents to give me a white leather Bible to carry to church on Sundays and Wednesday nights when I attended Girls Auxiliary meetings—we held an official title abbreviated as the GAs.

Then there were Junior Choir practices and practices for the Christmas play. I starred as Mother Mary one year and even forgot my lines for one nerve wracking hot minute before God and everyone else in the sanctuary. (I know I've told that story a thousand times. Peyton loves to say, "Mom, you repeat yourself." And I say, "One day you will be just like your mom.") However, it was traumatizing, so deserves to be retold because therapy wasn't a thing back then and my red cheeks burned for days because I didn't portray the divine momma of Jesus the way she should have been portrayed. I doubt Mary ever forgot her lines. She never even thought of saying "no" to an angel telling her she would be the mother of the Christ child. She had the best comeback.—She simply asked what all women ask for: details.

But back to celebrations: The family celebrations rolled around along with songs played from the stereo like, "Rockin' Around the Christmas Tree," "Blue Christmas," and "Another Tender Tennessee Christmas" and Alvin the chipmunks begging Christmas to hurry up and don't be late. "Alvinnnn!"

Groaning tables made room for more casseroles and desserts that enticed passersby as they strolled along weighing the merits of meringue and the horror of more thigh dimples that were a sure sign of possible future deleterious diabetes.

Mother baked everyone's favorite pie or cake, and my request was invariably Red Velvet. Mother always made the best Red Velvet Cake I've ever eaten. So moist and slathered with a cream cheese icing loaded with pecan pieces. Since there were pecans on that cake I vowed and declared it had to be healthy eating.

And now, it pains me to think about it, but Robert Kennedy, Jr.—a certified health nut in the best kind of way—is getting rid of food dyes that are harmful to my health. Red dye is on his hit list. One time, just one time out of the year red dye is used for our Red Velvet Cake and now Bobby has to go and ruin one of my family's Christmas traditions.

Geez, Bobby. I seriously doubt baking a double layered cake with red dye in it once every Christmas season is going to kill me. Will I and my descendants never get to pass that recipe down to children not yet born? Will those future kids never get a chance to taste really excellent and moist Red Velvet Cake?

Will red dye ever be sold on the black market to people like me longing for just a slice—one measly thin slice—of Red Velvet Cake? Will I never again get to say that word that vibrates my lower lip when I say it? Red Vvvvvvvvel-vet.

I now picture myself flying to China to buy red dye from a girl who flashes her spy-looking trench coat open—the same Chinese girl I saw on social media during the Covid pandemic opening a black trench coat with rolls of toilet paper taped to the inside as she walked the streets looking to meet up with people also walking the streets searching for the toilet paper she was selling. Cash changed hands. Or maybe it was a couple of gold bars. Not long after that, toilet paper could not be bought in a grocery store anywhere in the USA. Remember? Shelves were empty. Some folks were hoarding it in their bath tubs, closets, and laundry rooms.

My daughter and her husband were soon to purchase a new home, and after arriving at the showing, they saw one small room designated for the extra rolls of toilet paper. An entire room! Piled to the ceiling! So that's where all of the toilet paper ended up. Embarrassing! And to think there might be people out there having to revert to using lamb's ear from the garden, or ancient Sears and Roebuck catalogs, or old newspapers or....

And would you now make me become that person who will be hoarding all of the red dye so I can have Red Velvet Cake for Christmas dinner? You betcha, Bobby!

And then it hits me. Something I'd never thought about before. That Red Velvet Cake represents the blood of Christ that was shed for sinners like me. Why had I never associated the Red Velvet Cake with the sacrifice Jesus made for us all? Even the people who didn't yet believe in Him? And why didn't that pop into my mind all of those years Mother served Red Velvet Cake for Christmas, and afterwards when it was my turn to make the cake until I passed the baton to my daughter?

And she'll pass the Christmas-cake-making tradition down to her three girls. Will they even be able to find red cake coloring in years to come?

Oh, me. That Red Velvet Cake is such a big deal, I even bought a special white cake platter stand in San Francisco for my daughter when she and her husband lived there for a year before returning home to Tennessee via a year's stint in Denver. Will that white cake stand simply be used for doughnuts from here on?

I shudder.

It's sacrilegious just thinking about not having a Red Velvet Cake on that white cake stand.

I know Robert Kennedy, Jr. is only trying to help us get

healthy again, *But Bobby, you're turning my Christmas's upside down. I can't think about Christmas without a Red Velvet Cake!*

And then I think about poor lowly Jesus, having to die for all of us. He knew why He'd come to Earth. He knew what His mission was. His mission wasn't about Red Velvet Cake and toys. His mission was all about pouring out His red blood to save the lost, like the sinner on the cross who at the last possible minute believed Jesus was who He claimed to be. The Savior. Willing to go through the most horrid death ever thought up by mankind. The cross. Jesus knew what He faced. And the burden was so great He sweat agonizing drops of blood. The sins of the entire world were upon Him, He who had never sinned. The One and Only Son of God who'd never done anything wrong—sent to save us.

And here I am thinking Bobby's so righteous about taking my red cake coloring from me—love you Bobby—that I haven't been able to see the proverbial forest for the trees all of these years until now. I'm trying to get my mind wrapped around my not being able to have a piece of that traditional Red Velvet Cake recipe.

But if I have to do without it, so be it. I suppose I'll have to give up Diet Dr. Pepper as well. Aspartame is such an ugly sweetener that does not like brain cells. And Coca-Cola recently put liar-liar-pants-on-fire satan's name on their cans. *Fix that too, Bobby, while you're at it!*

I guess there also goes Mother's famous Dr. Pepper Cake recipe—the one with fudge icing she always beat with a spoon resoundingly clanging against an iron skillet to make Daddy's favorite Christmas cake. I could never beat cocoa and sugar et al into the right consistency for the necessary two solid minutes like Mother could for the cake's icing. Like a tennis player who can also serve a volleyball over the net with force, I suppose all of that switch pudding Mother served up to me when I was a child helped her arm never tire so she could beat chocolate and sugar into Dr. Pepper Cake icing or fudge if she beat it a minute longer.

I digress.

If aspartame from Diet Dr. Pepper eventually gives me Alzheimers, maybe I won't remember I ever had Red Velvet Cake during Christmas. Lord Jesus, just please don't let me forget about you!

Maybe from here on out, I can bake a totally white cake. White represents the white mules and horses kings rode in ancient times. White also represents the white robe I'll be wearing once my filthy rag is discarded and I'm made new and all cleaned up to take my heavenly place with the rest of the saints who have passed on. I pray my new body has no sagging parts. If necromancy wasn't frowned upon by God, you'd better believe I'd be trying to contact some of my friends up there asking about "the new body." And if they made it. If they made it. I hope all those sinner-saints repented and made it.

Back to the cake. Perhaps my family can make white cake the new tradition. And instead of drinking Diet Dr. Pepper, I can switch back to regular—the same Dr. Pepper version Mother used. That means hitting the treadmill again and exercising along with dieting. Ewww. Why did I have to use exercising and dieting in the same paragraph?

Whatever the new traditions will be, I'm just thankful I still have a bottle or two of Red Food Coloring for now. But wait, I can always make a run on the grocery store and store those new bottles in the cardboard rolls in my toilet paper room so I'll have a long-lasting supply. Did I just tell on myself?

If I'm lucky, perhaps the rapture will happen before I run out of Red Food Coloring. Either that, or perhaps I can sell some of that Red Food Dye on the black market street corner while I'm wearing a black trench coat lined with little glass bottles meant for bringing Red Velvet Cake back onto its rightful cake stand. If I have to die because of dye, I won't go out alone. There will be a herd of people going out with me because we Southerners do love our Red Velvet Cake…and keeping our hair roots from showing.

Could someone who has Bobby on speed dial please tell him to go easy on us when it comes to the red dye—Southern traditions die hard. You can have your yellow and orange—I don't mind you taking those dyes away—but that red, that particular color will not go easy into the night!

And don't get me started on hair dye, honey, because if Bobby goes after that coloring, the South will surely rise again and I don't mean from baking red cakes using Martha White. I'm talking full out war because no Southern grandmother who has yet to go "all out gray" can show up at the school Christmas plays with gray roots teasing out her real age.

Can somebody get me Bobby on speed dial? I need details!

The birth of Jesus is primarily described in the Gospels of Matthew and Luke. To read these stories go to Matthew 1:18-25 and Luke 2:1-20.

~ 18 ~

Stained Glass Ornaments

Mother once said to me, "I miss Mama and Daddy. I no longer have a 'home' to go home to." I replied, "But Mother, you still have me."

"It's not the same," she said. "It's just not the same when you don't have a Mama and Daddy and a 'parent home' to go home to."

Daddy piped up, "I miss the old folks."

After my parents left this world to go to their everlasting home where they are waiting for me, I at least still have a special place and special friends I visit. Pete and Kathy. To go to their log cabin home and spend time with them is like going home for me. Pete has always been like a big brother full of knowledge on so many subjects—always there with a helping hand when I need him. He's helped cut down trees for me and solved my computer problems more times than I count. If it weren't for Pete's encouragement and insistence I get an author's website up and going, I doubt if I'd ever have ventured onto the internet. His firm, "No, I'm not going to keep up your website for you, you must learn to do the work yourself" stung at first. I'd been stuck back in my college days of, "I abhor writing code in computer class" and didn't want to leave my stuck place. What was easy for someone who taught computer classes around the world and wrote articles for IBM magazine was difficult and boring for me. Reading one of his IBM articles was like reading jibberish. Pete's patience, prompting, and emboldening "you can do it" talks paid off. I finally launched my website and my work has been read by people in at least 120 countries around the world.

Pete's wife Kathy—one of my dearest friends I've mentioned before—and I have not only traveled together, we've been creative together. I've always loved creating things whether it be sewing, knitting, crocheting, needlepoint work, macramé, liquid drape dolls, smocking, pottery or artwork.

Years ago, Kathy shared recipes with me that she'd created. She also taught me how to make beautiful sheets from a dreamy material we used to buy, and how to weave baskets the Native American Cherokee way. The most recent craft she taught me a few years ago is how to make stained glass Christmas ornaments.

A trip to Pete and Kathy's house begins with a wonderful iced tea to sip while visiting on the long front porch. We catch up on the latest and then Pete helps with taking my luggage up the stairs into the loft of their log home.

I walk back in time as I step into a living room that reminds me of an 1800s movie set. The entire upstairs suite is filled with antiques. Kathy's stained glass pieces enhance every window while almost every Louis L'Amour book published resides in a bookshelf that I've frequented on multiple occasions.

Back downstairs, I give Lucy the cat a scratch behind both ears before a delicious supper is placed steaming hot on the table. After Pete and I both vote for sausage and biscuits and gravy for the next morning's breakfast, we chat before the fireplace—if it's chilly enough—until bedtime.

The next morning, after a big breakfast, church services, and a visit to the Apple House atop Dayton Mountain, Tennessee for winesap apples, Kathy and I go to work. Behind the log cabin home is a smaller studio cabin where Kathy creates her stained glass artwork. After showing me the pieces she'll soon be soldering together for a long rectangular window to go above the double doors of the church where she and Pete attend worship services, it's time for me to choose my Christmas ornament patterns and decide on the colors of stained glass I'll be using. In the past, I've made angels for my granddaughters along with Christmas trees, ball ornaments, and a candlestick holder with a yellow flame.

This time, and for a young niece and two young nephews, I choose a different angel pattern, a Christmas tree, and a Santa face. Now I step over to where the large sheets of stained glass are kept in slots and bins Pete built for Kathy. The smaller pieces—scraps from bigger projects—are kept in labeled plastic containers. "No scrap is ever thrown away," says Kathy. "Never know when a small piece might be used for a hand or a foot, etc."

Once the stained glass has been chosen—some whites have swirls and are beautiful for angel wings—patterns are traced and the cutting begins using a pistol grip oil-feed glass cutter. Many cuts are made because tracing around curves in a continuous movement doesn't bode well. Best to make the cut on past and away from the curve off the stained glass. After a cut has been made, the use of the tapping ball instrument from underneath the stained glass piece helps to free the glass to be cut from the main glass.

After all pieces have been cut, its time to put on protective eyeware and go to the grinder to smooth off the rough edges.

Each step, if done properly, makes the work easier when it comes to the next step—which is wrapping narrow copper foil strips over the edges of the cut pieces. This is the most time consuming and tedious step, but it must be done. Once the foil is on, both edges of the foil are bent over the glass pieces on both sides and a burnishing tool is used to make sure the foil strips are smoothed down, adhering to the glass.

When the foil wrap has been completed, it's time to solder the pieces together. On a board of wood with a lip nailed across the bottom and up one side to hold pieces firmly and prevent them slipping off of the board—that was also designed by Kathy and assembled by Pete—the pieces are assembled to look like the finished pattern. The nails—horseshoe nails are best for this next job because they're flat on both sides near the sharp points—are hammered in around the pieces to hold them in place so they don't move during the initial soldering process.

Next, a stained glass flux, a clear liquid, is brushed over the copper foil so the lead—usually 60 percent tin and 40 percent lead—can be used to solder the copper foil seams where the pieces touch each other. Once the flux has been applied and the soldering iron has been heated to between 361-376° F, the soldering can commence. If one is right handed, the lead is held in the left hand and the soldering iron is held in the right hand.

Once the seams have been soldered together, the nails can be removed so soldering the rest of the copper foil edges of the ornament can be completed.

After all of the glass pieces have been soldered together, it's time to solder a metal ring at the top of the ornaments so ribbon can be threaded through the ring for hanging on the Christmas tree. Then once that last step is finished, it's time to clean up the ornaments. When dry, it's necessary to recheck the seams and edges of the glass to make sure the lead has covered and filled in where every speck of copper foil is showing. If not, back to the soldering iron and lead step for touchups.

I've hit the highlights of making stained glass Christmas ornaments. Once into it, there are certain nuances that can only be learned from hands-on experience. Like making sure the seams aren't "flat." Or, that there is enough melted lead to give a rise or small bump to the seams. Learning how to position the soldering iron so rolling pieces of lead can "be grabbed" back to the iron to use in other needed places comes with time and practice.

But once the ornaments are finished and each one has been placed in a bubble wrap envelope with hand-written notes on the outside to each child, the joy comes when I see their little eyes light up as they open their early Christmas gifts.

And giving a homemade keepsake Christmas gift that will last long after I'm gone back to heaven to be with my parents is special. I cherish Christmas keepsakes from my family and when my grandees and great nephews and niece are grown and have children of their own—that's one way of them keeping my memory alive every year they come across those stained glass ornaments to once again hang on another year's tree. Hopefully, they'll not only remember the reason for the season—Jesus who died to save them—they'll also remember me—a grandmother to my grandchildren, and to my nephews and niece, a Great Aunt who loves them like my Great Aunt Ruby and Uncle Tommy loved me.

~ 19 ~
The Nutcracker Saga

The Tivoli, Chattanooga's "Jewel of the South" and one of the country's picture palaces, is an essential, thriving part of the fabric of Chattanooga. After two years of construction and almost $1 million spent on its high-domed ceiling and grand lobby that boasts crystal chandeliers in the Beaux Arts style popular for movie palaces of the 1920s, the theatre was opened in March of 1921. A $30,000 Wurlitzer organ was installed in 1924. And in 1926, the Tivoli became one of the first public buildings in the nation to be air-conditioned. Just standing outside to purchase a ticket must have been thrilling back in the day—long before Ticketmaster came into being.

It's been written that one hundred years of memories live within the Tivoli Theatre's walls. I have so many of my own memories of the grand dame of Chattanooga that reside in the Christmas memory files of my brain.

After the birth of television, the gorgeous Tivoli fell on hard times and into disrepair. I well remember the talk floating around the city about the Tivoli's possible demise and the possibility of the theatre being demolished. Broke my heart as a tender child. I would always remember cold winter nights, Christmas shopping downtown and walking past the Tivoli's doors and peeking into the lobby to view the magnificent stairs that led to the balcony. If only I could walk up the right side of that grand double staircase to descend on the left once more.

Thanks to Chattanooga's Benwood Foundation, the theatre was saved and placed on the National Register of Historic Places. Then in 1986, the State of Tennessee, the city of Chattanooga, and the Lyndhurst Foundation funded a $7 million two-year restoration, and the Tivoli has been a significant and important part of Chattanooga's cultural, entertainment and arts scene from then on.

It was on the Tivoli's stage that I once danced alongside friends from my dance class, and also where I once saw Madame Butterfly flit across between the curtains and before those in the orchestra pit who played their music from below the front row lights. The Tivoli is also where I first heard country singer Faith Hill sing, as well as many other artists.

Not only did I attend plays and operas performed at the Tivoli, I also heard well-known Southern writers and authors speak there. And later, I would attend an award ceremony for my dear friend's young son whose writing showed promise. To see that young man walk across the Tivoli's stage to accept his writer's award was a special day. I was honored to be a part of that family's celebration. And I especially enjoyed hearing The Chattanooga Symphony perform on that hallowed stage—my violin instructor was one of the violinists who taught at the University of Tennessee at Chattanooga's Cadek Conservatory of Music and helped make the Chattanooga Symphony magic happen.

But what I remember most about the Tivoli is the Christmas Nutcracker performances. The first one I attended was in the 1970's—Mother had made her first two granddaughters matching burgundy outfits to wear and I was helping her get the little angels to their seats. Later in the ballet, Mother and I whispered to each other and agreed that overall, the ballet could use some work. Mother said, "But we don't have to tell anyone and the girls have never been so they don't know any different!"

Years later, when my daughter Peyton was interested in being a Nutcracker mouse, all had changed. Those putting on the ballet had upped their game. The performers were of a different caliber. What made the difference? Practice, practice, practice. All ran smoothly and the practices were held every Saturday for months at Baylor School at the foot of Signal Mountain.

Hair had to be pinned up in a bun with a protective net covering before hairspray was added to make sure not one wisp escaped. Tights had no runs. No way was a practice to be missed if it could be avoided. All of us moms with dancers had no life once Nutcracker practice began.

I'll admit, I was better at being a "tennis mom" because I didn't have to deal with allergy issues if I'd had boys playing baseball in the dirt and grass. What I really enjoyed most was being a "Pony Club Mom" (I didn't care one whit about dirt and grass and allergies then because I loved equines.) rather than a "Dance Mom" because I was better at pulling a horse's mane than I was at putting up the perfect human bun. Plus, horse's were my passion—so allergies from hay and grass was something I dealt with. However, a "Dance Mom" I became so my mouse could wear makeup and whiskers and surreptitiously prance across the stage.

During the finale of the big weekend performances leading up to Christmas, moms put heads together and planned a big feast of finger foods and sweets and drinks to be placed on long tables in the huge dance studio that was also used as a dressing room and hangout when the dancers weren't on stage. I always volunteered to bring the Nutcracker cake. Not only did I not have to deal with the logistics of baking such a cake, assemble it, and then ice it, all I had to do was pick it up from Jackson's Bakery and pay for it. Big win!

Then there were the flowers to buy to be presented at the end of the performances. I overheard conversations that went like this: "Did you pick up the flowers?" "No, I forgot the flowers—did *you* pick up the flowers?" "Why do mice have to receive flowers?" "Hush now, it's a tradition for those who perform to receive flowers after their last performance of the weekend!"

Horses didn't need flowers—horses were happy to get carrots or hay. I always remembered to pick up the hay even if I had to haul a couple of bales in the trunk of my car if I wasn't driving the truck.

The next year, Peyton was one of the polichinelles—children of the humongous Mother Ginger who could run beneath her enormous skirt. The outfits were yellow with red polka dots. Since Peyton was one who could perform a decent cartwheel, she had the privilege of cartwheeling herself across the Tivoli's stage. I must say how grand it was to watch the performance up close and personal from a private box seemingly floating in midair near the stage. I'd always wanted to sit in one of those private boxes for a performance when I was younger, and the polchinelle-cartwheeling year was finally my year. One time would do me.

The next year, I was relieved when my child decided to drop dance and pick up violin classes when she wasn't involved in Pony

Club or sports. Was the Nutcracker stage fun? Yes, for a time it was wonderful, although harried, fun and missing the University of Tennessee football games was no big deal because I could do without the Knoxville weekend ballgame traffic jams.

When granddaughters arrived, I thought surely my grandees would want to join in on the Nutcracker fun. There was interest there for awhile with Hayden. But dance lessons weren't her jam as the kids say. Her dream of being a mouse in the Nutcracker like her mom had once been, faded.

However, her dream of standing on the stage at Christ Church in Nashville with the children's choir and also the adult choir singing Christmas hymns finally came true—which was much better than being a mouse. I'd much rather a grandee be on stage as a beautifully-gowned saint singing Christmas hymns for the real King than on Tivoli's stage for being mice soldiers for the mouse king.

Psalm 30:4 NIV: *Sing to the Lord, you saints of his ; praise his holy name.*

~ 20 ~

The Scent of Christmas

I once cooked Brussel sprouts the day before my daughter and her husband's house showing. My son-in-love loves Brussel sprouts and so does my daughter, and I was only trying to please them. But what was I thinking? The odiferous smell of cooked cabbage lingers into the 'morrow like a drive-by skunk spraying.

Not only that, I used to hold a real estate's license and I, of all people, knew one is supposed to bake cookies—something that gives off a pleasant or pleasing smell that can sell a house and make the buyer long to live in that home. (A spaghetti dinner in the oven helped seal the deal on my first home!) That's just it—I wasn't thinking when I sautéed those Brussel sprouts! And Christopher has never let me live down my faux pas—after 15 years he still loves to tell about that ghastly "skunk cabbage" ambiance from years ago. And even though the joke is always on me in the telling of that story, I still sauté up Brussels sprouts for him on a regular basis.

However, during the Christmas holidays, I don't make the mistake of cooking any type of "skunk cabbage" unless I'm taking the dish to someone else's home with the stink—I mean aroma—left behind. Instead, I cook dishes that are pleasing to the olfactory nerves and fill a home with Christmas joy. I use cinnamon, nutmeg, vanilla, cloves, lemons and limes on the stove top to make the house smell divine. The smell of chocolate covered cherries resting in a candy dish has an especially satisfying and tempting flavor. And there's nothing better than the scent of a sugar cookie straight from the oven ready for a sugar dusting.

Fresh pine and cedar branches for fireplace mantels are also wonderful scents to bring into the home. The smell from a burning hardwood fire evokes a special memory. Lighting fir or vanilla candles is another way to disperse scents that remind me of the outdoors and fond trips to the woods with Daddy for a cedar Christmas tree. These are all surefire examples for helping a home smell like Christmas.

Sometimes I wonder, "God, have some of these wonderful aromas from down here wafted up to you yet? I know things seem awful down here with wars and rumors of war and the horrific things the human race is doing to one another as well as to the earth you created for us—but every now and then I hope You dwell more on some of our good and pleasing efforts to make You known by sharing about Your Son. P.S. Thanks for Your mercy and grace."

When I think on pleasing aromas and how I am made in the image of God, I also think about the verses in the Bible that talk about a pleasing aroma—incense if you will—when sacrifices were offered up to God:

Psalm 141:2 NIV: *May my prayer be set before you like incense; may the lifting up of my hands be like the evening sacrifice.*

2 Corinthians 2:15-16 NIV: *We are to God the aroma of Christ among those who are being saved and those who are perishing. To the one we are the smell of death; to the other the fragrance of life. And who is equal to such a task?*

Ephesians 5:2 KJV: *Walk in the way of love, just as Christ also hath loved us, and hath given himself for us an offering and a sacrifice to God for a sweetsmelling savour.*

Genesis 8:21 NIV: *The LORD smelled the pleasing aroma and said in His heart: "Never again will I curse the ground because of man, even though every inclination of his heart is evil from childhood. And never again will I destroy all living creatures, as I have done."*

Leviticus 2:2 NIV: *Take it to Aaron's sons the priests. The priest shall take a handful of the fine flour and oil, together with all the incense and burn this as a memorial portion on the altar, an aroma pleasing to the LORD.*

Leviticus 23:13 NIV: *...together with its grain offering of two-tenths of an ephah of fine flour mixed with oil—an offering made to the LORD by fire, a pleasing aroma—and its drink offering of a quarter of a hin of wine.*

Hebrews 13:15 NIV: *Through Jesus, therefore, let us continually offer to God a sacrifice of praise—the fruit of lips that confess his name.*

Revelation 5:8 KJV: *When he had taken the book, the four beasts and four and twenty elders fell down before the Lamb, having every one of them harps, and golden vials full of odours [incense], which are the prayers of the saints.*

But what about other fragrances? Our lives become a fragrant offering when we extend kindness, grace, and love to others. Our service and kind words—and when we give ourselves selflessly to help those who need our help—turn into a soothing aroma, a sweet fragrance that reflects the love of the One who gave His life to save us. We then become the hands and feet of the Lord here on earth taking care of our Father's business.

Sometimes we create a few messes and the aroma we send to heaven must smell more like "skunk cabbage" to God than a pleasing aroma. Hopefully, there is a next time and another opportunity and we can get it right.

God is all about second chances.

One thing I know, God is pleased when we put more emphasis on His Son than we do on manmade stories about Santa Claus and Nutcracker Mouse Kings. Celebrating the birthday of Christ and staying focused on Him throughout not only the holidays but also the entire year, has to be a pleasing and soothing aroma of cinnamon and other spices that God loves. (If God didn't enjoy the aroma of cinnamon, I doubt He would have used it in His anointing oil recipe from the Old Testament! Not only is cinnamon a healing spice, the aroma of cinnamon is a soothing aroma.)

And though we oftentimes get caught up in the busyness of Christmas—the shopping and baking and running here and there trying to make every party and go to every event—for me the best part of the holidays is going to my place of worship so I can truly give thanks and glorify Him with praise, songs, and worship. For if it weren't for God's saving grace and the offering made through His One and Only Son for the human race, there would be no holiday—no Christmas birthday to celebrate.

~ 21 ~
Santa's Big Question

It was time for the grandees to make the trek to see Santa Claus. Once in the room where Santa sat on his large chair next to Mrs. Claus, Hope looked leery but the bigs had their Santa request down pat.

Hayden said, "I want…and I want the American Girl doll Tenney's banjo and one of her outfits."

Santa said, "Well, well, well, every little girl is wanting Tenney's banjo this year. I'll have to check with the elves to make sure there are enough to go around. I'll surely see what I can do."

Then it was Harper's turn to sit on Santa's lap while little Hope clung to her mama's blouse for dear life. After Harper ticked off her list to Santa, he said, "Well, well, well. That's a pretty good long list. One thing I need to ask, have you girls been naughty or nice this year? You haven't been fighting have you?"

I stopped taking photos and sucked in my breath while thinking, *Oh no! That's the first time I've ever heard Santa ask that question. And no! They've had spats all year long. What in the world is Harper going to say?* I saw the wheels in Harper's mind turning.

She took only a few seconds before replying. "Well, Hayden had been wanting me to kick her for a long time!"

~ 22 ~
Christmas on the River

When I lived in Chattanooga, I accepted every invitation I received from my friend Tracy to attend her church's Christmas events. In Tracy's Methodist church, the choir dressed like angels and violins played in their orchestra. The music never failed to bring tears. God *had* to love instrumental music because He always put His singers and musicians before His warriors when they were off to battle, and the word for "songs" in the New Testament Greek is "kitharodos," which means to sing with musical instruments that are plucked. (The root word of "kitharodos" is *kithar*, from whence our English word "guitar" was derived.)

Then, back in the day, another dear friend, Kathy, always invited me to her little country church on Suck Creek where the music was equally as good and sweet—just different. There on the river banks, a violin was also played and those playing hadn't been gone from their heavenly home all that long. Some of the musicians were the children and young grandchildren of the preacher. Their sweet and precious voices were heavenly.

Now I'll share something with you. Sundays at Suck Creek wasn't high church. Let me paint a clear picture: Suck Creek is a boulder-rugged place running through the Appalachian mountains that loom dark and verdant and smell of pine, cedar, and wild honeysuckle tangles above the Tennessee River. The area got its name from The Suck—the place in the river that had such a strong whirlpool it sucked boats under for years, until they smoothed out the devil holes with dynamite. It was located above white roiling rapids called "The Pan" and "The Skillet."

During their wilder days for a short time after WWII, my hellion uncles from Alabama on my Daddy's side ran moonshine down Tennessee's Suck Creek river road trying to survive the Great Depression while beating out starvation. Many Southerners of Scot-Irish descent made their own whiskey to cut a bad cough because they couldn't afford doctors and town medicine. The money they made from selling whiskey put shoes on their feet and their children's feet and supplied the basics if a crop had failed due to drought. It took a long time for the Great Depression government to notify the South that better days were around the bend. Times were difficult.

My church-going uncles from Alabama on my mother's side probably prayed for my other uncles' deliverance or wished the devil would send them to hell—one of the two, because whiskey and white lightning had a mean bite that could destroy some men who were tempted to regularly imbibe even when they weren't ill and needing to cut a cough.

On one occasion, when Mother was pulled over for a traffic ticket, the city cop asked her if she was kin to the rowdiest uncle, J. D. Mother knew when the city policemen couldn't manhandle her brother-in-law to jail, they'd call the state troopers in for backup. So, Mother white lied and said no, he wasn't kin (meaning by blood), and prayed God would forgive her later. She was terrified the policeman would jack up her fine to help ease the wounds J. D. had inflicted on the officer of the law's head the week before.

Eventually, God brought those rowdy bad-boy uncles to their knees and they were delivered. The Lord works in mysterious ways, especially when southern women know how, and how often, to pray. God has a way of taking the frisky out so He can hand-smooth our wrinkles. But it took a coon's age for them to completely dry out. Like sponges, they had to be wrung a few times, put through a couple of washing machine spin cycles, and sun dried.

But back to The Suck. I'd heard a few crusty stories about the place. The people who lived on The Suck were sometimes evil and violent. In some cases hard times made for hard people if they weren't acquainted with Jesus. Violence and the devil were all they knew, conditioned like Pavlov's dogs, drooling for their white lightning when they heard the souped-up whiskey runners' cars. Used to, you had to be pretty tough to drive through that neck of the woods yourself.

Now, however, things were cleaning up down that road. There were some nice homes and good-hearted people building out that way. Of course, there were still some hold-out families entrenched, hanging onto squalor, which is what they felt they had to defend. Either that or meth labs. One guy staked out pit bulls around his dilapidated trailer to scare people off. He waved his gun at his new preppy neighbor. Preppy started waving his new gun back.

I'd heard the guy's Mother shot her husband and killed him—stone hammer dead. When she died, another son went down to clean out her trailer while his brothers took pot-shots at him. "Duck and weave" was their trademark. However, there were good, God-fearing poor people living on The Suck, too.

As I drove down Suck Creek Road one December Sunday morning, I topped a hill. The vista before me took my breath. It was the same view ancestors would have seen when steering flatboats to what is now Alabama while fighting an Indian scalping. That part of the river had seen buckets of blood spilled throughout the last few centuries. Now, the river rolled between two mountains and the anticipation of Christmas wafted in the air. I tasted living water through the smell of wood smoke, and recalled Mother saying she was baptized in an Alabama creek and Daddy was baptized in the Tennessee River. I couldn't help but burst into song:

> Let's go down to the river to pray
> Studying about that good ol'way
> And who can wear the starry crown
> Good Lord, show me the way.
> Oh, sisters let's go down
> Let's go down, don't you wanna go down
> Oh, brothers let's go down
> Let's go down to the river to pray.

The small country church I was visiting sat almost at the water's edge. Next to the white building, my tires crunched onto the gravel parking lot as I searched for a parking spot.

Once inside, I sat next to Kathy and Ruth, always on the fourth row back, knowing those two were always prepared with their pieces tucked away in their purses. Just in case.

Kathy used to have a second river home on the Suck. Ruth lived there fulltime. Though they hadn't grown up there they knew a lot more than I did about the territory and its people—including the solved and unsolved murders. I'd never known a time when either gal didn't pack heavy metal, since some parts of Tennessee had yet to be tamed.

Jake sat on my other side. He'd just returned from Iraq, broken in spirit, unable to return for a second tour. He was hoping God would honor his desire to attend medical school—felt he was being called. He'd seen enough dead, mangled bodies and felt the Lord was leading him to bind and heal instead of maiming and killing. His scars ran as deep as the river running beside us.

A Harley rider showed up—we could hear him before he entered because his motorcycle's vibrating rumble announced his arrival. Dressed in a purple shirt with a black leather vest and black leather britches, he wore a cross necklace on a gold chain. He sat in the back. At one point he stood and said, "The fields of heaven are a brilliant color, like nothing you've ever seen."

All eyes turned to gaze at him. His countenance radiated truth that beamed out over the pews.

"The angels sing like you can't believe. I spent time with them after my aneurism burst and sprayed brain matter on the ceiling of my car. Jesus said I couldn't stay. I had to come back and tell everybody about the message; that dying was nothing to fear if you believe He can wash your sins away with His crimson blood."

Then there was Brother James who continued with the sermon. He drove an hour every Sunday from the city to preach a beautiful message with no fire and damnation antics like I'd witnessed in some country churches. He preached with love and tears in his eyes when he talked about the Savior's sacrifice. I was moved when I saw he was truly Spirit filled. He picked up his mandolin. His two daughters sang while his five-year-old granddaughter picked up her violin, which was called a fiddle down on The Suck. Slater played acoustic lead guitar and Clemmons sang bass and played base guitar. Colby played drums and there by the river with the boats nestled nearby we sang:

> And He said: Rise and follow me
> I'll make you worthy
> Rise and follow me
> I'll make you fishers of men.

> And He said:
> Peter, John, and James
> Could never be the same
> After they heard him say
> I'll make you fishers of men.

There were no plates passed, nor hats. Some gave their widow's mite into a slotted wooden box on the way out the door. Most didn't have a widow's mite to give but you could tell their hearts were right with God even if they were battling a cancer, the loss of a loved one, or heartrending loneliness. There wasn't one adult in there who could say they'd never wielded a shield. Most of us had fought, bled, laid down and slept, only to rise the next day to pick up our swords to fight again.

From the churchyard, some of us went to Clemmon's home

where he and his wife lived upstairs. Part of the downstairs had been turned into living space for elderly men—some dying and previously homeless. A few were younger and still working. We watched the smiles on their faces as they opened our gifts.

Finally, I could put a face to the name I'd drawn from a bowl a couple of weeks before. As I looked at the man before me, Rusty, I was reminded of how the prophet Isaiah described the coming Messiah: "He had no beauty or majesty to attract me to him, nothing in his appearance that I should desire him. He was despised and rejected by men, a man of sorrows and familiar with suffering."

I watched Rusty's weather-worn face tilt upward as his broken smile broadened when the K-Mart steel-toed work boots he'd put on his Santa list fit. And I saw hope in his shy and humble grin as he looked up at me in thanks. It was then I glimpsed a light flickering in eyes that had seemed defeated moments before. And in that second of a heartbeat, Rusty gave me hope in return.

I was thankful God had blessed me so I could bless Rusty and hopefully, Rusty's faith would expand, growing deeper—knowing that God provided by way of other's human hands when a man was down on his luck and couldn't provide for himself.

I realized for the umpteenth time that God has a way of bringing His children together. The good Lord had shown me how to be more than a Southerner washed in water. He showed me how to be washed in the blood, a true fisher of men.

When I think back on that Christmas, I'm reminded of the Prayer of Jabez: *Jabez was more honourable than his brethren: and his mother called his name Jabez saying, Because I bare him with sorrow.*

And Jabez called on the God of Israel, saying, Oh that thou wouldest bless me indeed, and enlarge my coast [territory], and that thine hand might be with me, and that thou wouldest keep me from evil, that it may not grieve me! And God granted him that *which he requested* (1 Chronicles 4:9-10 KJV).

That Christmas, Jabez's prayer had become mine. God's hand was with me as He enlarged my coast and led me into a territory I'd never have ventured into before by myself because I'd always feared the stories about The Suck. The good Lord kept me from evil so I could gift Rusty with a present he needed for work but couldn't afford to buy himself.

My gift in return was not only Rusty's smile and appreciation, I'd also been gifted a gift from the Harley rider who had meandered in while traveling the country to tell us his precious story about the angels he heard in heaven and the message Jesus had for us; "…that dying was nothing to fear if you believe He can wash your sins away with His crimson blood."

Now that, my friends is the true meaning of Christmas and why we celebrate the Christ child, the Saviour He became, and His birthday. And what a sweet and joyous birthday party it is!

NOTE: All names but Ruth and Kathy have been changed.

May You Have Many a Merry Christmas
And May Your Christmases Be Bright!

If you liked this book,
please leave a book review on Amazon.
Thank you in advance!

About the Author

Vicki H. Moss is former Editor-at-Large and Contributing Editor for *Southern Writers Magazine* where she interviewed authors and contributed articles on writing in addition to blogging for the magazine's Suite T blog. She also wrote a weekly column as a pundit for the *American Daily Herald*. As a workshop instructor for writing conferences, Vicki teaches from her books *How to Write for Kids' Magazines* and *Writing with Voice*. With over 850 articles published, she co-authored the book *Nailed It!* and contributed to Cecil Murphey's book, *I Believe in Heaven*. A poet, blogger, speaker, free-lance editor, and ghost writer, Vicki is frequently on faculty as a workshop instructor along with school author visits. She's also author of *Southern Grandmother Stories, Adrift, Smelling Stinkweed, Rogue Hearts,* and two poetry books *Roisin Dubh* and *Porch Pickin' People*— and always has a work in progress. Writing for many venues, she's published articles and poems in Scotland's *Thistle Blower, Country Woman, Christian Devotions, In the City, Hopscotch, Fun for Kidz, Boys' Quest,* and has written over 40 stories for the *Moments* series published by Grace Publishing.

    www.livingwaterfiction.com
    Instagram @vickihmoss
    X @VickiMoss

www.ingramcontent.com/pod-product-compliance
Lightning Source LLC
Chambersburg PA
CBHW070457100426
42743CB00010B/1653